An Illustrated History of

Limavady

(Léim an Mhadaidh)

and the Roe Valley

from Prehistoric to Modern Times

GW00471316

Douglas Bartlett

Published by Douglas Bartlett
©2010 Douglas Bartlett

Designed by April Sky Design, Newtownards
(www.aprilsky.co.uk)
Printed by GPS Colour Graphics Ltd, Belfast

ISBN 978-0-9565683-0-4

Front cover photograph: The Broighter Gold, a collection of gold
artefacts that were found near Limavady in 1896.

Contents

to Odile

Acknowledgements

I WOULD LIKE TO thank my three children Tara, Ryan and Manon for their heart warming support and encouragement as I worked at this project. Tara was involved in the important early stages, reading through the content for me, with a critical eye. As the book progressed, my younger daughter, Manon, was often called upon to rectify errors caused by my careless computer skills and she helped out with research, on occasion too. Ryan has not only taken many of the photographs featured in the book, but has also spent many long hours painstakingly proof reading the final draft.

Big brother Graham and my good friend Hunter McClelland, also proof read the work for me, checking it with a reassuring thoroughness that is rarely found these days. In addition to proof reading, Hunter also took the time to improve the quality of many of the images used in the book, some of which were in need of upgrading.

I owe my greatest debt though, to my wife, Odile. Her drawings, photographs and advice, pepper the content. Through her help and interest alone, she merits the book's dedication several times over.

Photographs/graphics/artwork credits

The Bridgeman Art Library, Reverend J. Blair, T. Candon (by kind permission, copyright photograph of Ulster History Park and with acknowledgement to Omagh District Council), Father M. Collins, D. Corr, Limavady Community Development Initiative, photograph (former Limavady Workhouse), J. Cowan, Environment and Heritage, "Crown copyright, reproduced with the permission of the Controller

8

of Her Majesty's Stationery Office", photographs/illustrations (old Banagher, Bovevagh, Drumachose and Walworth Churches, Ancient Cross, Dungiven Priory Chancel, O'Cahan's Castle, Audley's Castle, Watchman's Hut, Reconstructed Rath), D. Forrest, Reverend H. R. Given, D. Harper, Father O'Hagan, R. Irwin, D. Larmour, photograph (Burning of Lundy), Limavady Borough Council, (C. R. Phillom's 1699 map loaned by B. Brown), J. Lueg, McCausland's Drenagh Estate, photograph (Drenagh), Canon S. McVeigh, Manor Architects, photograph (Moneymore model Plantation village), D. Miller, photograph (The Lodge) National Museum of Ireland photographs (The Broighter Boat and The Broighter Hoard "These images are reproduced by kind permission of the National Museun of Ireland"), The National Trust, photographs (The Rough Fort, Martello Tower, by kind permission), The Newry and Mourne District Council, photograph (John Mitchel statue, by kind permission), Northern Newspaper Group, North West Independent Hospital, photograph (Church Hill House), Penguin Books: front cover of The Red Pony by J. Steinbeck, reproduced by kind permission, Penguin Classics 2000, W. Purcell, Public Record Office of Northern Ireland, permission granted by The Deputy Keeper of Records for use of various maps/illustrations (Ballykelly, Dungiven, Ballycastle, Limavady, Phillips document and Limavady Canal), Roads Service, 'By permission of the Royal Irish Academy copyright RIA', drawings (three flanker towers, Walworth Bawn), J. Simpson, photograph (Thomas Nicholl taken by Reverend T. Simpson), Ulster Museum, (Largentea Pottery, Dungiven Costume, photographs reproduced courtesy the Trustees of National Museums Northern Ireland), Ulster Folk and Transport Museum images and photographs (Duncrun Cottier's House by kind permission), Reverend A. Wilson, Western Education and Library Board.

The author has made every effort to find copyright and to acknowledge copyright where it is known to exist, but would be pleased to be made aware of any omissions.

This book is supported by Limavady Borough Council

and has been given financial assistance by The Honourable The Irish Society

Introduction

THE PAST HAS LEFT its mark on the area in and around Limavady. In deserted locations, ancient stones, once set down by Prehistoric people, can still be found, almost undisturbed by the passing of the centuries. Here and there the ruins of early Christian churches can still be traced, lying quietly in out-of-the-way corners. Celtic ringforts and the later Plantation settlements too, go remarkably unnoticed, in a region steeped in history.

This book is intended to serve as an explanation and a reminder of the history which still survives about us in our Borough. It takes the story from the earliest of times to the start of the 20th century, and places Limavady into the context of the wider world. The significant contribution the Roe Valley and its people have made to that wider world is highlighted. From the missionary, to the politician and on to the revolutionary, the area has fostered more than its share of figures who have each, in very different ways, made telling contributions on a broader canvas. The Drumceatt Convention alone would be enough to make the area important, without the Danny Boy heritage or the Broighter Gold, and yet that leaves aside Ritter's early hydro-electric development in Limavady, the exceptional musical gifts of Denis O'Hampsey and the local connections with John Steinbeck, to mention but a few aspects. This modest little town is the centre of a region that has made an important impact on more than just Irish, British and European History. It has an undeniably impressive past that glitters with significant artefacts, figures and places, all along its story. This is indeed, a past worth sharing.

The Prehistoric Period

The First Inhabitants

CURRENTLY THE EARLIEST EVIDENCE we have of people living in Ireland comes from a site on the banks of the Bann at Mountsandel, Coleraine. These people, from the Mesolithic period, were hunting and gathering their food in and around the Mountsandel area, some time between 7,900 BC and 7,600 BC, or well over 9,000 years ago, in other words. Their ancestors are thought to have arrived here from northern Britain, by crossing the land bridges or narrow seas that existed then. They had chosen their site well. It provided a year-round supply of everything needed to survive.

The River Bann and the open seas nearby were teaming with salmon, flounder, sea bass and Lough Neagh eels, all of which could be harpooned in season. Autumn provided a plentiful supply of nutritious hazelnuts, crab apples and water lily seeds to eat. Sailing out of the Bann estuary they could easily find a valuable supply of flint, either close at hand in the area around Portrush, or a little further along the coast in the other direction, at Downhill beach. The precious flint was then skilfully shaped into the spear and arrowheads essential for hunting the wild pigs that roamed around the Mountsandel locality. Trapping the over-wintering wild fowl, such as widgeon, teal, coot and capercaille, along with eagle, goshawk, red-throated diver and songbirds,

Left: Limavady's location in relation to known Mesolithic sites

added further variety to the diet of these early Irish people.

While these people were semi-nomadic, shelter became important, particularly during the winter months. Research initially carried out by the archaeologist Dr Peter Woodman in 1976 and further substantiated since, found that huts were built there at four different times during the site's period of occupation. They were simple huts built by driving saplings into the ground in

Below: Mesolithic hut reconstructed in the former Ulster History Park

a rough circle.

These saplings were then bent over and lashed together to form a domed roof. Lighter branches may have been interwoven to add strength and rigidity before this was covered with bark, or perhaps deer skin.

Grass turfs lifted from inside the shelter were then used to further protect it against the biting north winds. The huts were around six metres wide with a bowl shaped hearth in the centre and were capable of housing up to a dozen people.

These people may well have had as much free time as peoples living in more 'civilised' societies. Indeed it is very likely that they found the time to practice their own particular rituals and beliefs and art forms, though nothing of this has yet been retrieved in Ireland. Similarly, although these first known Irish people were living only a short distance from the mouth of the river Roe and the Roe Valley, no direct evidence currently links the area around Limavady to these Mesolithic people.

The First Farmers in the Roe Valley

There is, however, a clear connection between the Roe Valley and the early farmers who came to Ireland. Around 3,500 BC, family groups began arriving in Ireland by sea with their domesticated pigs, sheep and cattle, in the period known as the Neolithic, or New Stone Age. In order to find grazing for their animals, they quickly opened up the extensive forests that they found here. We know they were able to fell trees very effectively with porcellanite axes, but they may well have used a variety of methods, including setting fire to the trees, or ringbarking them. When the pastures they created were no longer of use, the animals were simply moved on and the same process was started all over again somewhere else.

Although there were relatively few farmers, it is easy to imagine how their methods had a heavy and immediate impact on the landscape at the time and also indeed on the semi-nomadic hunters and gatherers who might have been searching for food in the area. However, these original inhabitants, the Mesolithic people, would still continue their semi-nomadic lifestyle for some time to come, living side by side with this new farming community.

The newly arrived farmers quickly established a settled way of life here. They built houses and burial places, kept cattle and grew crops, and began trading goods such as pots and axes. One of the oldest known examples in Britain, or Ireland, of a house from this period, has been found at Ballynagilly near Cookstown. It was a rectangular dwelling, six metres by six and a half, made of split oak logs set upright in trench foundations and with post supports, which possibly held up a thatched roof. Similar houses from the same period have been found in central Europe and it seems Ireland was becoming one of the new destinations for people beginning to move steadily westward. Excavations in 2002/3 to build the by-pass around Limavady turned up evidence in the Killane area, of a seven metre by four metre Neolithic site. A few small post-holes and pits were found in one corner of the site. Flint artefacts, dated to around 3,000 BC, were found, as well as a hammer stone and an anvil stone. It would seem that there was a small building, perhaps a wooden hut with wattle walls and a thatched roof, on the site. This would probably have been occupied on a seasonal basis, in the summer months or early autumn, when these Neolithic people went fishing for salmon and eels in the nearby river.

This settled lifestyle meant that these people were able to learn new skills and would eventually make their own distinctive 'Ulster' pottery style. Some corn was now grown in Ulster, though cattle were of prime importance and had to be protected each night in a stockade from predators like wolf, bear, fox and lynx. With the hard, dense, porcellanite rock only being found at Tievebulliagh near Larne and on Rathlin Island, specialist axe factories grew up at these two places, in this period. We know that porcellanite axe heads were exported from both sites to places as far apart as Dorset and Inverness. Perhaps, in trying to cut through the dense forests of oak, hazel and thorn in the Roe Valley around 5,000 years ago, a farmer or two was lucky enough to be using one of the highly polished and much prized porcellanite axe heads that had been made at Tievbulliagh or on Rathlin Island.

However, there is more substantial evidence than that of the presence of these first farmers in our area. The practice of building burial sites for their dead was evolving in this period and we are fortunate to have surviving examples of these in and around the Valley and its hinterland. Several types of burial tombs were built across Europe, but Carnanbane Court Tomb, near Banagher Old Church, is an example of the 'court' grave type found most prominently, and almost exclusively, in the north of Ireland. This particular 'court' grave had two chambers with an east facing 'horned cairn' entrance made of small stones. There was probably a Neolithic settlement near the site, as these tombs were generally situated on or near fertile ground.

The largely unknown and neglected chambered grave at Carrick East situates these people deep in the floor of the Valley of the Roe itself. This latter site was excavated in 1936 and revealed six pottery vessels, including round bowls, which were typical of the sort of goods left with the dead in Ulster in the period. Enough of one pot remained to allow it to be restored. It was a simple round-bottomed bowl 7.7cm high, 7.6cm in diameter and 5-6mm thick. The bowl was decorated to a depth of 4.7cm from the rim with six irregular horizontal grooves, 1mm deep. Flint pieces and scrapers were also found in the tomb. Carrick East is described as a possible 'court' tomb by archaeologists, but to date, despite excavation, its central irregular oval with opposing single chambers defies a more precise classification. There are many examples throughout Ireland of burial tombs which come from the same period as Carrick East. The 'court' cairn at Audleystown in Co. Down, where the bones of thirty-four people were found, is one of the most impressive examples of a burial site in the north that dates from this time. Newgrange, in the Boyne Valley, is a unique and spectacular example of the sheer scale of the building projects that these people could undertake. It was, in essence, the same

Carrick East chambered grave

'Beaker people' pottery found at Largentea, Limavady

people who were to be found clearing the forests and establishing farms for themselves in the Roe Valley.

Another type of burial site, the type known as a 'wedge' tomb, is also to be found locally. These are particularly interesting because of what they tell us. Examples of these, such as those at Kilhoyle and Boviel and the hill-top burial on Carn Top, when taken along with the stone cairns near Largentea Bridge and at Gortcorbies on the Keady Mountain, show our ancestors using the high ground along the Sperrins, from the Benevenagh escarpments to the Keady Mountain and Benbraddagh through to the Glenshane Pass. 'Wedge' tombs were commonly used across different periods of settlement and the 'wedge' tomb at Well Glass Spring is especially important. Excavations undertaken in the 1930's, of the three-chambered tomb at Well Glass Spring, revealed the remains of six adults, a twelve year old child and an infant, a flint scraper, and sherds of a distinctive 'Beaker people' style pottery. Similar fragments of this pottery were found in the area of the stone cairns near Largentea Bridge, and at Gortcorbies. 'Beaker' pottery is more usually associated with the people who lived in the later period and this signals the presence in our area of people who could work with a new material, metal.

The Metal Workers

The use of metal in Ireland seems to have come about some time around 2,000 BC, as part of a very gradual change in lifestyle. On a second site, uncovered at Killane during the construction of the Limavady by-pass, coarse pottery fragments and flint artefacts were found in an area measuring ten metres square. There may also have been a timber building on the site dating back to between 1,500-500 BC, in the Bronze Age period. A piece of copper waste, or slag from copper smelting, was discovered in the larger of two hearths revealed during the excavations, suggesting that the hearth may have been part of a furnace. Burnt deposits further supported this idea, as they seemed to indicate the line of the flues radiating from the hearth.

Copper was the first metal worked, but later it was alloyed with tin to make bronze axes, cauldrons and small items like pins and fasteners for adornment. In the neighbouring Sperrin Mountains, gold could be panned in the streams, just as it still can to this day -though to a much lesser extent! Gold, like copper, was also used to make dress pins, and fasteners. Rings, bracelets and highly elaborate neck ornaments known as gorgets and lumulae were also produced at this time.

From around 500 BC a new metal, iron, was introduced to Ireland. The metal workers of this period are renowned for the unique artistic style they created which delighted in distinctive, highly decorative and intricate patterns. They are equally known for having brought a considerable military element into our society, while on the practical level, the iron tools they manufactured allowed these people to cut the forests even more effectively and to be able to establish simple farmsteads in the lowlands and valleys.

The King's Fort and the Rough Fort

The Rough Fort on the outskirts of Limavady and the King's Fort near Drumsurn, are two highly prominent and important examples in our area of these defended farmsteads or ringforts.

Situated just below the summit of Donald's Hill, in the townland of Kilhoyle, and overlooking the hamlet of Drumsurn, the King's Fort is one of the best preserved raths in Ulster. Positioned to use the natural defences offered by the terrain, it is protected on its south side by a steeply falling slope and it has an impressive ditch on its north side, with a bank around six metres high. As well as having a moat, the rath had souterrains, or man made tunnels and it is thought that in addition, the outer enclosure of the King's Fort may have been planted with thorny scrub such as gorse or blackthorn, giving its inhabitants even more protection. The souterrains or tunnels would have led to chambers in the defences or to 'escape hatches' outside the rath. The location and scale of the rath would suggest its owners were once important and influential people in the

The King's Fort, Drumsurn

area, people of status, in what was at the time, a warrior-led society.

While it has been estimated that there were over 40,000 of these defended farmsteads in Ireland, much fewer now remain and fewer still are as prominent and as well preserved as the Rough Fort, situated on the edge of Limavady town.

Although such sites are often called 'forts,' they are more properly known as raths and would have been home to an extended family which would have farmed the adjoining land. Some raths survive as slightly raised platforms and some were paired or grouped as the need to expand arose. The banks of these raths were normally of raised earth, though where it was readily available many were faced with stone, or indeed built entirely of stone. Occasionally the banks had a palisade that gave added security, but the defensive structure seen at the Rough Fort was probably as much for protection against wolves as against humans. Cattle had a special significance for these people, being used as a means of measuring a person's wealth and status. Consequently the cattle would have been brought inside the palisade of the rath at night to prevent them from being stolen or attacked. The trees that now ring the Rough Fort and give it a picturesque and imposing aspect were not planted until a later century. The 19th century Ordnance Survey

Memoirs record the rath as once having been the property of Marcus McCausland and state that he was responsible for planting a white thorn hedge on the site in addition to fir, oak, sycamore and birch trees. It was also noted that the man charged with taking care of the 'growing timber' was given a free house and garden. The practice of planting trees on such sites was fashionable during the late 1800's when tourism was becoming popular and it was considered more appealing to the eye to landscape them in this way. It seems there was also a fence built around the rath by Mr McCausland in this same era and that an 'aged man,' known locally as Kane of the Fort, held the key to the gate.

In 1931, six urns, some bones and a piece of a bronze knife blade were found in a cist a few paces away from the rath. The urns were broken on removal, but the pieces were sent to Belfast to what is now the Ulster Museum. The ancient rath, currently under the care of the National Trust, retains two distinct outer rings which protect the inner living area. A causeway that leads into the centre is easily recognised and it is not difficult to imagine yourself back in time when standing inside this particular 'farmstead.' Houses would have been round or rectangular, and built of timber, wattle and daub. Some would have had a porch, a hearth and a chimney. In a few cases the whole rath may

The Rough Fort, Limavady

Artist's impression of a rath in use.

have been thatched. A rath would have been home to a family and probably some servants. Often too, there would have been outbuildings where carpentry and metalwork were carried on and iron axes and ploughs were made. In and around the rath, livestock were raised and cereals were grown. Ringforts are most commonly found in the lowlands where the forest was being cleared to make way for a growing population. Most were built between 500 AD and 1,200 AD and some were used right up until the 19th century.

The Rough Fort does not seem to have had souterrains, or man-made tunnels like those of the King's Fort. Impressive structures, well-preserved and prominently sited, the two very contrasting raths, taken to-gether, give us an illuminating glimpse of a distant past which is difficult to equal. While the importance of the King's Fort has been given wider public acknowledgement with its recent inclusion in the North Sperrins Heritage Trail, the Rough Fort remains as yet, under-exploited in the Roe Valley area as a feature worth visiting.

The Broighter Gold

Aside from raths like the Rough Fort and the King's Fort, another distinguishing feature of this period is the quality of the gold goods produced during it. One of the finest examples of a collection of gold articles ever found in Ireland was discovered just outside Limavady, in the townland of Myroe, an area which borders Lough Foyle. The find, which became known as the Broighter Gold, was discovered in February 1896 by Thomas Nicholl when he was ploughing the land of his employer, Joseph Gibson.

The discovery became the centre of a celebrated court case between the Royal Irish Academy and the British Museum. The courts were asked to decide whether or not the hoard had been deliberately hidden in the area for later recovery. If so, it could therefore be classed as 'treasure trove.' If, on the other hand, the hoard had been cast into the sea as a 'votive offering,' it could be sold privately, would be acquired by the British Museum and would in effect, leave Ireland. The well-known barrister of the time, Sir Edward Carson, was involved as counsel on the side of the Royal Irish Academy, which eventually won the case.

In 1903, amid great controversy and interest, Justice Farwell assigned the hoard to the National Museum of Ireland in Kildare Street, Dublin, as 'treasure trove.' The judge was eventually convinced that since ancient sea shells found near the hoard were proven to pre-date the hoard, the gold goods must surely have been hidden there for later collection. Justice Farwell's pronouncement at the time is worth recording:

> *"The court has been asked to assume the existence of a votive offering of a sort hitherto unknown, in a land where such offerings were unknown, in a sea not known to have existed, to a sea god, by a chieftain, both equally unknown."*

A modern court however would most likely take the opposite view and accept that the hoard was more than probably thrown into the Lough Foyle basin as a 'votive offering' to Manannan Mac Lir, who was our Irish version of the god Neptune. The hoard consisted of a large, highly decorated gold collar, a gold necklet, two gold chains, a golden bowl and a small boat of beaten gold, which had a mast and yard, seats, fifteen oars and a boat hook and rudder. An exact copy of the find was displayed in the Roe Valley Country Park exhibition area in recent times, and a hologram re-creation has since been put on permanent display in the town's Tourist Office. The actual collection though, still remains in the care of the National Museum in Dublin. While the collection holds a relatively low-key position in terms of promoting the town, the Broighter collar alone is significant enough to be used on the reverse of pound coins, as part of the regional symbol for the province. The boat features on the Republic of Ireland's millennium Euro, and it has appeared on a series of stamps issued by An Post. The Broighter collar image was also used in this series of stamps. It is an outstanding treasure and we are very fortunate that the Broighter Gold, the King's Fort and the Rough Fort provide us so readily with such important and tangible evidence of Limavady's Iron Age past.

Thomas Nicholl

The Broighter Gold is characteristic of the Celtic La Tene style of decorative art. The Celts were the first people north of the Alps to emerge into recorded history and the collar, with its intricate swirling patterns, provides us with a clear indication that they had arrived in Ulster well before the start of the Christian era. Their La Tene art style, which takes its name from a site in Switzerland on the northern edge of Lake Neuchatel, typically comprised spirals, symbols and round patterns. As a style, it was a complete contrast to the classical realism and natural beauty that had been preferred by Greek and Roman artists. By 500 BC the Celts dominated the northern half of Europe and in 390 BC, took Rome itself. There is no clear evidence though, to tell us when the Celts came to Ireland, nor when they arrived in Ulster.

Their civilisation seems to have filtered into Ireland from Britain and the European mainland over centuries, gradually bringing their language and lifestyle here. On horseback and equipped with iron weapons, they brought the native people under subjugation. As well as their decorative art, the occupation of large hilltop enclosures, like Tara and Emain Macha (Navan Fort), is also typical. The Gaelic civilisation that emerged in early Christian times was a blend of language, belief and tradition that would survive in Ulster for centuries to come.

This was not to mean the end of Roman influence over Europe however. The Roman Empire grew once again, extending this time, as far as Britain. With this expansion, Ireland too came under threat. In 82 AD, the Roman General Agricola gathered his fleet into the Solway Firth for an invasion of Ulster. The distinguished military commander and governor of Britain intended to end his career with another notable conquest. News of a Pictish rebellion and the mutiny of German troops stationed in Galloway, however, required a change of plan and Emperor Domitian ordered him north into Scotland.

The Broighter Gold

Ulster would not be invaded.

Subsequently Ireland was little touched by Roman civilization and culture. It seems rather to have managed to maintain, even into the 17th century, an aristocratic Iron Age society, not unlike that of Gaul as described by Julius Caesar. Unfortunately for historians however, there is little to tell us about this period in our history. We are forced to turn to the epic tales of the Ulster Cycle which, while being enthralling in themselves, are unreliable as history, as they often intertwine mortals with magic at the expense of fact. The earliest versions of this, The Cattle Raid of Cooley, written down in the 8th century, form the oldest vernacular epic in western European literature. Whether it reflects life in the 1st, 5th or 7th century AD or even if it records actual events, is not certain. Tribal names from this period have still some resonance today though. The Cruithne, or Cruthin were the most numerous people in Antrim and Down. Locally they gave their name to Duncrun in Magilligan, meaning 'fort of the Cruithne' and to Drumcroon near Coleraine, meaning 'ridge' or 'hill of the Cruithne.'

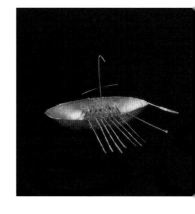

In the 4th and 5th centuries legion after legion was withdrawn from Roman Britain in order to defend Rome from the attacks of groups of German-speaking people coming from central and northern Europe. Left exposed, Roman Britain came under attack from the Picts in the north, the English from the east and the Irish from the west. The motives behind the attacks on Roman Britain differed depending on the group. Some sought to create new kingdoms, some were after loot and some were looking for slaves. A large hoard of decorated Roman silver from Ballinrees near Coleraine may well have been plundered from Roman Britain in one such raid. Around the same time a young slave called Patricius, known to us as Patrick, was captured and brought back from a raid. As Roman Britain was crumbling, he, more than anyone, would ensure that Roman civilization would profoundly affect Ireland from that day until the present.

2

The Coming of Christianity

The Missionaries

St Colmcille and Drumceatt

PATRICK WAS NOT THE first, nor the only missionary, to bring Christianity to Ireland. He was, however, the only one to have left a written record, The Confession. This document is taken as marking the beginning of written Irish history. Most places associated with Patrick are in the northern half of Ireland and it was probably in Ulster that he did most of his work. Here, as elsewhere, Christianity put the Celtic gods to good use. Existing festivals were incorporated into the Christian calendar and ritual sites such as Armagh, Tory Island and Derry became significant centres of the Church in Ulster. The sacred oak groves frequently used by the druids were particularly favoured sites for building monasteries and churches. It was not by mere chance that Patrick's disciple, Colmcille, founded his great monastery in the area known as Doire (Derry), meaning 'oakgrove.'

St Colmcille

After the death of St Patrick in the middle of the 5th century, the work of Ireland's monasteries and missionaries was, in later centuries, to earn the country its reputation as 'The Land of Saints and Scholars.' The work of St Colmcille, from Gartan in Donegal, would do much to help establish this reputation in subsequent years. He personally, would emerge as one of the greatest of all the saints of the era. Colmcille had many connections with the Limavady area. These ties seem to have begun in his youth when he was a frequent visitor to a church founded by St Patrick at Duncrun, Magilligan. Indeed he is said to have blessed the ferry crossing he regularly took from Donegal, ensuring that no one would drown on this stretch of water - which is good news for the present day ferry operators going between Donegal and Magilligan. The major turning point in the life of St Colmcille, or St Columba as he is also known, came in 561 AD with his involvement in the battle of Col Dreimne. It is said that Colmcille had copied a psalter without first asking permission. When the matter was debated, the judgement went against him:

"to every cow its calf, to every book its copy"

As far as the clan of the high-born Colmcille was concerned, it seems it was excuse enough for conflict. In the ensuing battle 3,000 warriors were said to have lost their lives. As penance, Colmcille decided to exile himself from Ireland by leading a mission to the island of Iona in Scotland. During this period of self-exile however, he did much to redeem himself by establishing a highly renowned monastic settlement and mission on Iona. The great reputation he gained through his work on Iona was to lead to an invitation to return to Ireland in 575 AD to preside over the prestigious Convention of Drumceatt.

The Convention, held on the raised mound of Mullagh Hill, situated behind the present day Radisson Hotel, was of great importance in deciding the future of relations between the Scottish and Irish Dalriada. For more than a century these territories on both sides of the North Channel had formed a single kingdom. In the middle of the 6th century however, Bruide, King of the Picts, posed a threat to Scottish Dalriada. The Convention came to the decision that the Scottish Dalriada should become independent, though with an agreement that they would help their tribal cousins in times of trouble.

Mullagh Hill

The future role of the bards in Ireland was also to be decided at the Convention. Wandering the country in 'companies' and carrying their Pot of Avarice with them to collect offerings of silver and gold, the bards had become such a nuisance that it was proposed to banish them from Ireland altogether. In its wisdom the Convention decided to safeguard the rights of the bards, but to curtail their growing excesses. It was agreed to reduce the retinue of a major poet to twenty-four, and that of a minor poet to twelve, thus ensuring that their all-important cultural knowledge and skills would be protected. The Convention's decisions then, had not only strengthened the Dalriada Alliance, but also secured the place of the bards in Irish society. It was said that Colmcille had played a major part in the debates, arguing particularly convincingly to protect the position of the bards and the oral tradition.

The significance of this, and indeed of his return to Ireland, would not have been lost on Colmcille. As he stepped onto the banks of the Roe, he must have felt honoured and fortunate to have been invited back home to offer his counsel. It is perhaps for this reason that it is claimed that he wore sods on his feet, so keeping his promise, never to touch the earth of his native land again.

Colmcille is believed to have returned several times to Ireland subsequently and is said to have established a monastery in 584 AD, near the site of the church founded by Patrick at Duncrun in Tamlaghtard Parish, Magilligan. The monastery's site appears on the 1831 Ordnance Survey Map, where it is described as the 'Ruins of an Abbey.' An important related Ancient Stone, inscribed with a double Cross, still stands undisturbed on a local farmer's land. An article in the Royal Society of Antiquities from 1903, says that when a Bishop Reeves visited the Cross some

The Ancient Stone inscribed with a double Cross

time towards the end of the 19th century, the foundations of a small building, thirty-five feet by nineteen feet, were also visible. As recently as 2001, the local historian, Jim Hunter, writing about the area, said traces of this building could still be seen. The fact that the foundations are still around is noteworthy, while the survival of the double Cross into the 21st century is as remarkable as it is reassuring.

Colmcille is also credited with having founded the Church of Screen in Ard Magilligan. With the passage of time the Church of Screen fell into ruin and the construction of the Limavady to Coleraine railway in the 19th century led to its location being further disguised. A plaque located near to the former Magilligan Station now marks the church's approximate site. He is also associated with a monastic site at Bovevagh founded in 557 AD and is also said to

Left: Plaque marking the approximate site of the Church of Screen

Below: Bovevagh Old Church

have founded an Abbey in 585 AD at Tamlaght, Ballykelly. Colmcille placed his friend St Findluganus or Fion Lugain over this, as its first abbot, and though it was no longer an abbey by the 13th century, and was in ruins by 1622, the name Tamlaghtfinlagan is still very much alive in the locality. Colmcille died on Iona at the age of seventy-seven. The date has traditionally been taken as being 9th June 597 AD, and it is celebrated in the religious calendar as Whit Sunday.

St Canice

Born in Drumrammer, on the outskirks of Limavady, about 516 AD, St Canice is less well known than his close friend St Colmcille. He is, though, worthy of singling out in this period in his own right. Canice, or Cainneach as he is also called, studied under Finnian at the monastic school at Clonard and became renowned for his deep study of the scriptures. His studies continued under Cadoc of Llancarfan, near Cardiff, where he was ordained as a priest before returning to Limavady. As Canice was of Pictish origin, Colmcille invited him to join him as a missionary in Scotland. Canice went on to spend ten years in Scotland, where his name is remembered as Kenneth in several place names, such as Inch Kenneth off Mull, and where he is also remembered as the founder of churches in Coll, Tiree, Mull and South Uist. On his return to Ireland he founded monasteries at Kilkenny and Aghaboe. It is accepted that Canice died, in or about 600 AD, in Aghaboe, on the 11th October. It is said that a row ensued over his coffin, between the men of the Aghaboe and the men of Kilkenny. The tale goes that while the two parties fought, a second coffin miraculously appeared. This ended the row and allowed both parties to go home with a coffin each. However, since Kilkenny prospered from that time on, and Aghaboe declined, it is held in popular myth that actually the Saint's body was borne off to Kilkenny.

In the local area, the ruins of the old church at Drenagh on the Coleraine road, mark the ancient site where, around 550, he established the church and monastery of Drumachose. In the townland of Ballycrum, which borders Drumrammer, a well, known as St Lowry's or Lurach's or sometimes as St Canice's, is said to have special healing powers. It is claimed that it

St Canice (stained-glass window, Christ Church, Limavady)

Drumachose Old Church

was here that St Canice was baptised by St Lurach. The Ordnance Survey Memoirs of 1834 recognised the healing powers of the well and detailed how this worked. It seems that before a person could be cured of an illness or disease, the two trout in the Well had to appear to the afflicted person. The affliction could then be left behind by leaving a rag or piece of clothing on a nearby tree. These places often hold an enduring power and attraction for people and until recently it was also the custom to bathe young children in the Well.

Canice's name is still used locally as in St Canice's Faughanvale Parish Church, Eglinton and Termoncanice Primary School, Limavady, for example. Although it is little known or referred to nowadays, Canice also remains the Patron Saint of both Dungiven and Limavady.

St Aidan

Aidan is another saint from this illustrious period who is connected with the area. Like Columba and Canice before him, Aidan chose to leave Ireland to become a missionary for Christianity. He rose to fame as the great Saint of Lindisfarne, and when he died it is claimed that St Colman brought back his remains to Ireland in 667 to their present site in Tamlaghtard, Magilligan.

St Aidan's grave

It seems that the remains found their way here somewhat fortuitously. Following a ruling by the Synod of Whitby in favour of the Roman Church over the Celtic Church, Aidan's successor, St Colman, determined to found a new religious house in Ireland. Blown off-course on his way to Mayo, Colman arrived at Magilligan with several of the bones of the venerated saint. Feeling he had been guided by God and having been impressed with the devotion he saw in Magilligan, he built a cairn in the area and deposited Aidan's bones.

The cairn was near the site of a much-revered local well which was believed to be capable of curing all ills. Capitalising on these ancient traditions and superstitions, Colman blessed and dedicated the well and its healing powers in the name of St Aidan. Subsequently, in order to obtain a cure at St Aidan's Well, the sufferer, then, as now, had to take dust from the cairn where Aidan's bones lay. For the cure to work, the dust,

St Aidan's Well

mixed with the well water, then had to be applied to the afflicted spot and an offering left at the well. The church there was later re-dedicated to St Aidan and his grave/cairn has a prominent place in the cemetery.

It would be wrong to think that all the finer biographical detail of the lives of the Saints would stand up to proper historical scrutiny. What is clear though is that for a long period of time the Roe Valley played a prominent part in the island's political and religious affairs, exerting an influence which extended well beyond the immediate locality. St Aidan, St Canice and St Colmcille have each made significant contributions to Christian heritage, not least in carrying on the missionary tradition of St Patrick. Clearly too, our community has every right be very proud of this worthy and important heritage.

The Vikings

The serenity of tranquil monastic life was soon under real threat, even here, in the Roe Valley. Little hard evidence can be found of the Viking attacks or settlement in the immediate area around Limavady, but folklore has it that Danes established a large fort on the north banks of the Curly Burn, at Dunmore, a short distance outside our present day town. There are tales too of raids on the shores of the Foyle and counter-raids on the Innishowen forts that the Norsemen had established.

Aed Findliath is said to have taken on and defeated the Vikings in a notable naval victory in 861 AD on Lough Foyle. The prevalence of the surname McLaughlin in our area, meaning son of Viking, hints at our Viking past. The ruins of a round tower at the site of the former abbey at Tamlaght in Ballykelly make a similar allusion to this period. While it is still uncertain what precise function round towers served, one purpose may have been to warn the surrounding population of imminent Viking attacks.

Unfortunately, these tantalising glimpses are all we have from the passage of the Vikings through our area. They seem to have had more success and interest in developing trading ports in places like Dublin, Wexford, Waterford, Cork and Limerick than they did here, in the comparative remoteness of the North-West.

The Clans of the Roe Valley

With the waning influence of the Vikings in the area, power fell into the hands of the local clans. Clan warfare was a major part of the backcloth of life at this point. The O'Connor clan dominated the Roe Valley for a time, but by the

The small Mortuary House in the grounds of Banagher Old Church

11th century, the O'Cahans had regained control. Their control over the area would remain right up until the 12th century, ending only with the coming of the Normans.

Christianity had an important role for these clans in this period. Banagher Old Church, for example, near Feeny, is thought to have been founded by the McLouchlainn chiefs in 1100 AD, and houses the relics of St Muirdeach O'Heaney in its Mortuary House. A carving on the front of the Mortuary House is most likely to be of the saint. Locally, it used to be said that sand from within the churchyard sprinkled over anyone or anything, from a solicitor to a racehorse, would bring good luck, particularly to those with the Heaney surname. The continued connection of the clans with Christianity is seen in the Augustinian Priory at Dungiven. Built between 1150 AD and 1200 AD, it was to become the chosen burial place of the chiefs of the O'Cahans, who had made Dungiven their stronghold sometime in the 12th century. The 13th century chancel, though in a ruined state, is regarded as the most impressive and accomplished work of its period in mid-Ulster. Its south wall holds the tomb of Cooey Na Gall O'Cahan, also known as 'The Terror of the Stranger.'

The main stronghold of the O'Cahans however was their fort on the banks of the Roe. Clearly marked in the present day Roe Valley Country Park, the site sits roughly a mile upstream from where the town of Limavady is now situated. It was from here that they would face the power of the Norman invaders who were to venture north from Carrickfergus.

Above: The 13th century chancel of Dungiven Priory

Below: The site of O'Cahan's Castle

The Norman Influence

Several Norman influences were seen in Ireland before 1169 when the first Norman knights came to our island. A number of Irish rulers had begun to copy Norman fashion in clothes and behaviour but their fighting strength would not be felt this far north until the arrival of John de Courcy. In 1179 AD, having established a settlement at Coleraine, de Courcy led an army through the Roe Valley, plundering the O'Cahan lands and churches. Using the monastic settlement at Derry as a base, he then continued into Innishowen. A shrewd campaigner, de Courcy realised the importance and influence of Christianity in Ireland and put the veneration of Irish saints to good use. In 1185, after his travels north, he claimed to have found the bodies of St Colmcille, St Patrick, and St Brigid in the rebuilt Armagh Cathedral, which he then renamed St Patrick's Cathedral.

Despite his prowess however, de Courcy himself was to be challenged by a fellow Norman, Hugh de Lacy. In 1205, Hugh de Lacy in turn invaded the O'Cahan lands defeating and slaying Feargail O'Cahan, the chieftain of the time. De Lacy eventually extended Norman control across North Antrim to take in both the Bann Valley and the Roe Valley. Erecting motte and bailey castles and setting up manors, the Normans went unchallenged until the battle of Down in 1260. As vassels, the O'Cahans were obliged to fight alongside the powerful O'Neills and with defeat in battle, the O'Cahans lost control of our region as far as Innishowen.

Norman influence increased as a consequence, and castles grew up such as Northburgh Castle in Donegal, built in 1305 by Richard de Burgo. Later to become known as Greencastle, it now sits as a picturesque ruin at the mouth of the Foyle. By 1296, when his sister Egidia was married to James, 5th High Royal Steward of Scotland, the area around Limavady was obviously considered settled enough for the castle and borough to be able to be offered by de Burgo as a wedding gift to the newly weds. Clearly the O'Cahan lands were well under the control of de Burgo by this stage. Known in 1333 to the English as Le Roo, the manor of the Roe was recorded as having two water mills where tenants could grind their grain, and a fishery on the river worth 20 shillings a year.

By the start of the 14th century the Norman influence was at its peak in Ulster. Richard de Burgo, the Red Earl, ruled with a firm hand. His children's carefully chosen marriages allied his family to other important characters of the day, including Robert the Bruce. He had extended his power as far north as Innishowen and had created towns of varying importance throughout the province. Coleraine vied with Downpatrick as his second most important town. It exported salmon caught at the Cutts and traded regularly with Gascony in France. With its fortified bridge, it was the forward position for attacks on the north-west. The borough of Limavady featured among the towns listed in the 1333 inquisition, or inventory. Though described as a town, in reality it was, like Belfast, Bushmills, and Portrush, little more than a village at this point. While the Norman presence was clearly in evidence, it was sparsely settled. The Irish were increasingly learning from the intruders and began to build stronger fortifications where their lordships bordered that of the Normans. With a Scottish threat to deal with in the north of England, the Norman influence in Ireland was gradually weakening.

The Revival of the O'Cahans

This decline in the power of the Normans was to be good news locally for the O'Cahans. They lost no time in taking advantage of the changing situation to re-establish their fort outside Limavady as their base. They also set up strongholds at Enagh Lough and Dungiven. A similar pattern was repeated throughout Ireland with Gaelic chiefs reasserting themselves, while the highly adaptable Normans integrated themselves into society by adopting Irish ways.

The Gaelic name for the O'Cahan kingdom was Ciannachta and although the kingdom no longer exists, the surname is still widespread throughout the north-west of Ulster in the form of O'Kane. The neighbouring O'Neill clan remained as their overlords. The usual obligations remained as well, such as having to pay a yearly rent of cattle and having to supply soldiers or kerne, when the O'Neills so requested. While the O'Cahans did not own the land they ruled, they were still able to lead the life of noblemen and did no manual work. The O'Cahan chief and his relatives spent their time hunting game and fighting wars. The wars were normally with their neighbouring clans but were sometimes fought against outside invaders. Scottish gallowglasses were regularly used in these wars to supplement the native Irish soldiers. Gallowglasses were well armed foot soldiers, 'picked and selected men of great and mighty bodies and cruel without compassion,' whose weapon of choice was a six foot long battle axe. Irish kerne each carried a short knife into battle, along with a small round wooden shield, and a bow and arrows. Not being of noble birth, the kerne took their orders from swordsmen. The chief was entitled to a tax from each farmer in the clan for the use of the land and this would have been paid in the form of cattle or corn. Normally a gathering of homes would have collected around the chief's castle or tower house, or around an important church or monastery.

Situated on an ancient pass through the north it is most probable that a cluster of unplanned homes developed like this at Dungiven where the O'Cahans had a base. The houses would have been made of mud and wattles, or in this case, most probably of stone since it would have been fairly readily available locally. Wattles were long thin rods cut from willow or sally bushes which grew along the streams. Roofed with a framework of willow beams thatched with rushes, these one-roomed homes had sometimes a hole in the roof to let the smoke out, but never a chimney. Rather inevitably they were dark and smoky inside. The surrounding townland or 'bally,' was farmed with the precious cattle kept close, apart from in summer when they were taken to the higher fresher pastures known as the 'bolie.' The area known as Bolea on the outskirts of Limavady retains this name to this day.

The castles or tower houses that the O'Cahan chiefs built were substantial buildings which were probably crude copies of 'keeps' built by Norman lords in earlier times. Often the only clues as to how they looked come from drawings provided by English artists in the 17th century. Surviving towers from the 15th century, such as Audley's Castle in County Down, can be invaluable as evidence, but it is known that styles varied slightly from region to region. The use of the two turrets linked by an arch, as in Audley's Castle, is unique to County Down, for example.

Audley's Castle

Tales of the Clans

Laura O'Donnell and Finn McQuillan

O'Cahan rule was often troubled by clan wars. There were bitter feuds between them and the neighbouring McQuillan clan. The O'Cahans could be found fighting both with and against the O'Donnells at various times in this period. One of the most famous feuds presumed to have taken place in this era was that between the combined O'Donnells and O'Cahans against the McQuillans in the 1540's. As the battle raged, Laura O'Donnell waited at a cross planted by the O'Donnells on the Limavady side of the old church at Drumachose. This area is still known as Crossnadonnell. She was hoping for news of the young man she had fallen in love with, Finn McQuillan, from the rival clan. As he was brought to her she noticed the white plume she had made for him dragging forlornly in the mud, and she collapsed and died of a broken heart. The two lovers were then buried together at Cairn A Finn, at Cahery, on the banks of the Curly Burn, where trees were planted to mark the spot.

Finvola

From roughly 100 years earlier, in 1428, comes another story that has been passed down to us through the ages, this time concerning the events surrounding the death of the beautiful Finvola O'Cahan. The story, which is associated with the Dungiven area, has inspired a much sung ballad entitled 'Finvola, The Gem of the Roe.' The tale behind the song relates how Finvola's family only agreed to her marrying a Scottish chieftain on the condition that she would eventually be buried in Dungiven. When Finvola died suddenly on the island of Islay, off Scotland, her family were unaware. They sensed a tragedy however, on hearing the cries of Granie Roe O'Cahan, the banshee that only cried for the death of an O'Cahan. Setting out for Islay the family found her husband crouched in grief over her grave. He agreed that she should be returned to her native Dungiven and with that the banshee was silenced. Harper's Walk in the town was the former site of a school for harpers and one of the most skilled of these harpers, Toal O'Cahan, is said to have been responsible for writing the tune that inspired the traditional ballad about Finvola:

> *"In the lands of O'Cahan, where bleak mountains rise,*
> *O'er whose brown ridgy tops now the dusty cloud flies,*
> *Deep sunk in a valley a wild flower did grow,*
> *And her name was Finvola, the gem of the Roe."*

Appropriately enough, Dungiven's premier international singing star of the moment, Cara Dillon, has recorded a beautiful version of the ballad.

The Legend of the Dogleap

It is in this period too that the town of Limavady is said to have been given its name. Legend has it that, in a dispute with their traditional enemy, the McQuillans from Coleraine, the O'Cahans found themselves besieged in their castle. In need of aid, the O'Cahans tied a message to the neck of a trusted dog, which was then released from their castle. The dog leapt the Roe at its narrowest point and ran off to bring back help from their Dungiven cousins. Help arrived and the clan was saved. In honour of the part played by the dog in saving his clan, the O'Cahan chief named the area Limavady, or Léim an Mhadaigh in Irish, meaning Leap of the Dog. To this day the town proudly uses the image of the leaping dog to represent it and this features too in its Coat of Arms.

The Irish Wolfhound was a favoured dog of the clans

The Legend of O'Cahan's Rock

The story goes that once when he was being pursued, an O'Cahan horseman leapt from this eighty foot high riverside cliff. He made it to safety on the other side of the Roe, landing on a rock. The imprint of the horse's hoof is still visible in the rock to this day.

The Town of the Ears

The Ballyclose area of the town gets its name from a rather gruesome tale of events that are said to have taken place in this period. It seems that two young boys were sent off to hunt towards the Largy wood, by the McCloskey clan. When the chief of the O'Mullans came upon them, he decided to drown the boys in the Roe. The next morning the McCloskeys took on the O'Mullans with the help of some of the O'Cahans. They were defeated and those of their number who were captured had their ears cut off

– Ballyclose means the town of the ears! The matter did not end there, however. Some of the O'Cahan clan had been away on a raid and when they returned there was another battle. The O'Cahans won this one and several of the O'Mullans had their heads cut off. The heads were buried at a place called Knock-Na-Ginn.

Many of these wonderful stories, and much more besides, come from the book 'Norman De Borgos', by Archibald McSparron, who was brought up in Flanders, Dungiven. His book has been popular since it was published back in the 19th century.

The Dungiven Costume

The Dungiven Costume however gives us clear evidence of the lifestyle of people from this time in history. This outstanding 'find' was discovered in Flanders, Dungiven, in April 1956, by a farm labourer removing a low turf wall beside the lane to William Dixon's farm.

The 'find' comprises a mantle, jacket and trews, or tartan trousers, and a pair of leather shoes. Initially the discovery drew little attention in the newspapers being captioned in The Northern Constitution under the simple heading: 'Coat and Trousers 356 years old.'

The jacket of the Dungiven Costume

The accompanying article detailed how it had been brought in one Monday to the Belfast Museum. Describing the importance of the items, the Director at the time, Mr W.A.

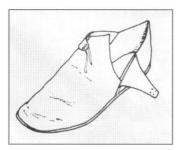

Typical 'brogues' worn from 17th to 19th century

Scaby, pointed out that the Museum already possessed a woman's jacket of similar date made of embroidered linen, but did acknowledge that the 'find' was "rare enough in Britain."

Later analysis of the custume showed that the clothes had been preserved in an acid, peaty soil. The conditions favoured the material but, had there been a body with this costume, the bones would long since have decomposed. The original jacket and trews were found to have been well made and elaborately finished, though they had been heavily patched at some subsequent point. The trews' tartan is woven in the Donegal fashion, in strips which vary in width and distance from each other, and they are in the style of those worn in the Highlands of Scotland at this time.

Although stained brown and tan, the tartan was probably a vibrant green and red colour originally with fine details in black and yellow. In the 1970's, the Scottish Tartan Authority registered it as Ulster Tartan and an American company, called 'Reconstructing History,' currently offers authentic pattern copies of the costume for sale. Following her research into how the costume was made, Kass McGann, the founder of 'Reconstructing History', has suggested that the original jacket was made for a man with a 42 inch chest. The shoes found with the costume were of the type known as 'brogues,' which were commonly worn in Ireland from the 1600's to the 1800's.

The area around Flanders belonged to the O'Cahans until 1641 when Manus MacCooey Ballagh O'Cahan lost his lands in the rebellion of that year and it has been suggested that the costume may have been worn by the O'Cahans of Antrim. There is though, no direct link to the costume with any specific group. It was dated to the late 1600's and was subsequently put on display at the Ulster Exhibition in November 1958. It is currently back on display in the newly refurbished Ulster Museum in Belfast. Along with the Kilcommon Jacket, found in Co. Tipperary, the Dungiven Costume forms a major part of the very small amount of archaeological evidence there is for 17th century Irish costume. It is indeed "rare enough in Britain."

3

The Plantation Period

SINCE NORMAN TIMES ENGLISH rulers had paid very little attention to Ireland. This and much else in Europe was about to change however, as the Reformation took hold. At first, Martin Luther's protestations seemed to amount to little more than the thoughts of a lone German monk and lecturer. Soon though, his searching criticisms were found to have touched a nerve and his ideas quickly evolved into a huge Reformation movement. It became a movement so important that it would challenge the Catholic Church's power and influence in the world and cause profound divisions across western Europe.

With Ireland remaining Catholic and England becoming Protestant, successive English monarchs would have to find ways to deal with the strategic threat posed by her near neighbour.

In a policy of Surrender and Regrant, Henry VIII tried to persuade the Gaelic lords in Ireland to come under direct rule, offering the inducements of a title and the right to own their land. After they had acknowledged Henry's authority, the powerful O'Neills of Ulster, for example, became Earls of Tyrone. During the 1550's, a policy of 'planting' people loyal to the Crown was tried out in areas close to The Pale,

Hugh O'Neill

which centred on Dublin. While this went some way towards protecting the English living there from the raids of the Gaelic Irish clans, the underlying issues in Ireland still presented England with an obvious threat.

On her accession in 1558, Elizabeth was soon made aware that she had inherited a small, rebellious and 'uncivilised' Catholic neighbour, capable of putting her very throne at risk. Despite Elizabeth having some control of large areas of Ireland, The Pale was still subject to attack and her foothold in Ireland was still vulnerable. In Ulster, the most difficult province of all, Hugh O'Neill chose his time well to launch the Nine Years War (1594-1603) against Elizabeth I.

The Ulster Plantation

After first seeming to be loyal to the new Queen, and accepting the title of Earl of Tyrone, O'Neill later began to rally the clans in the fight against English rule. A report produced for the English government noted that the local O'Cahans had sworn their allegiance to O'Neill at Coleraine, in June 1593.

> *"Randall McNeece, a Scott, stated that O'Cahan and his son did acknowledge Tyrone as their Lord, at Castleroe."*

It was reckoned that the O'Cahans provided 200 foot soldiers and 300 horsemen towards O'Neill's campaign during the Nine Years War. Indeed, during one of his most notable successes, at Clontibret in 1595, O'Neill may well have owed his life to an O'Cahan. According to Sir Hugh Lane, in a letter:

> *"Both were knocked off their horses and Sedgreve grabbed O'Neill around the neck. At that instant O'Cahan's son came to O'Neill's rescue and struck off Sedgreve's arm. O'Neill then stabbed Sedgreve under his coat of mail and killed him."*

With another victory over the English, this time at Yellow Ford near Armagh in 1598, O'Neill retained almost total control of Ulster. The following year Elizabeth spent a quarter of a million pounds on an army in Ireland, but it failed to bring the country under submission. In 1600 she appointed Lord Mountjoy to the task.

An experienced campaigner, Mountjoy planned his strategy well, including studying the geography of the land. He thought too about the location of O'Neill's allies, whom he set about trying to isolate. That way he could take them on individually, rather than face their combined strength. He planned a line of forts which the Irish would struggle to capture, because of their lack of heavy guns.

Lord Mountjoy

Mountjoy adopted other tactics which the local clans had not experienced before. Each time his men raided a settlement they carried away as much food as they could find and burned or destroyed the rest. While other deputies used to attack the rebels only in the summer, Lord Mountjoy regularly spent five days a week on horseback all winter long. This not only "broke their hearts", driving them from their homes and into the woods, but the endless need to keep on the move also "wasted" their most valuable asset, their cattle. Furthermore, the tactic made it difficult for the Irish "to sow their ground."

One of the most important differences from previous campaigns was the plan devised to attack the Irish on three fronts. Sir Arthur Chichester would harry the Irish from Carrickfergus in the east, Sir Henry Dowcra would attack into Innishowen and Derry in the west and Lord Deputy Mountjoy would push into rebel country from the south-east through the Moyry Pass. These tactics would cut the Irish off from each other and from their allies in Scotland and Spain. This time the English were intent on victory.

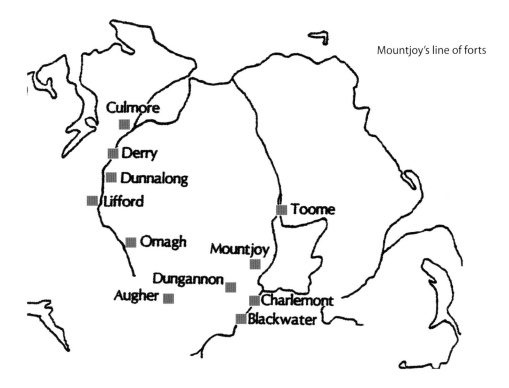

Mountjoy's line of forts

Dowcra in Derry and the Roe Valley

Sailing out of Carrickfergus on the 7th May 1600, Dowcra arrived at Culmore nine days later, with 4,000 foot soldiers and 200 horse troops. As the ships arrived they came under musket fire from the shore. By the 18th, Dowcra had captured the castle from Phelim O'Doherty and had left a garrison of 600 men there. He quickly moved on to take Derry, which fell, unopposed, on 22nd May.

Dowcra then decided to "sit it out all winter" and make Derry secure, rather than march directly into battle. Two warships were sent out to forage for timber across the estuary in O'Cahan's territory and "there was not a sticke of it was brought home but it was well fought for." Apart from attacking these foraging parties though, the Irish, by and large, left the English forces alone. The Irish in fact were few in number. The majority of their force had been drawn off by Mountjoy's diversionary attack, which had been specifically designed to give Dowcra time to establish a bridgehead on the Foyle. In any case the Irish were prepared to wait a little too, remembering how the previous garrison had been greatly reduced by insanitary conditions and by the gruelling weather in the north-west.

Dowcra was soon aware of the havoc the unhealthy conditions could wreak on his troops and why he had been given orders to build a hospital. His men fell ill "beyond expectation and almost all credit." They suffered greatly from the Irish weather and particularly from having to drink the local water instead of the beer they normally drank. Beer was quite often favoured over water as the brewing process removed the impurities in the water. Dowcra had experienced many a climate, but noted that the winter in Derry, and even more so, the summer in Derry, "made even my soul to grieve." Worse was to follow for Dowcra when he was struck on the forehead during an encounter with the Irish and for three weeks in July, was believed to be close to death.

In the wider campaign the Ulster lords, though still formidable, were now beginning to be on the defensive. The English mastery of the seas had cut off Scottish aid, while allowing the English to bring in reinforcements and provisions to bolster their war effort. Lord Mountjoy intended to bring the Irish to their knees. Burning grain stores and taking the Irish on in the winter, when it was difficult for them to hide in the leafless woods, was having an effect. In the winter of 1600/01, neither Mountjoy, nor Dowcra relaxed their campaign of attrition.

Important local Irish, first Art O'Neill, then Niall Garbh O'Donnell, began to join Dowcra's side against their own countrymen. Dowcra was to write that he depended greatly on the "intelligence and guidance" of O'Donnell in the winter months. The

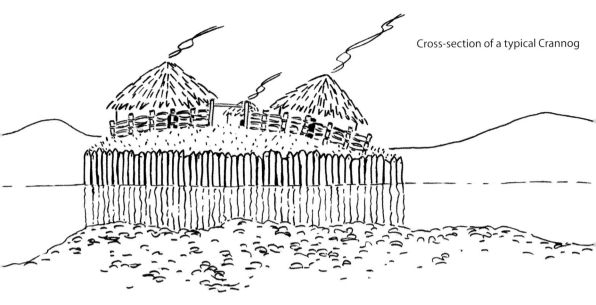

Cross-section of a typical Crannog

importance of drawing the Irish to his side was understood by Dowcra and O'Donnell himself later argued that Ireland had not been conquered by the English, but by his "own arms." Insistently, Mountjoy urged Dowcra to "burn all the dwellings and destroy the corn," by camping on it and "cutting it down with swords." With Derry under his charge, Dowcra set about harassing the local clans into seeking peace. In June 1601 he captured an O'Cahan castle established on an island on Enagh Lough. Having fortified the crannog, the O'Cahans had considered this stronghold as being very secure and Dowcra found it difficult to take initially. He had problems setting up the cannons, "for want of shovels and spades." After a whole day spent firing at the castle walls he was still unable to take the crannog and decided to move his cannon closer to the edge of the lake under cover of darkness.

In the morning Dowcra finally managed to occupy the castle, but found it deserted. The O'Cahans had slipped across to the mainland at midnight, secretly swimming ashore or escaping by boat.

Significant events in the wider war in 1601 went some way to easing the pressure on Dowcra's forces in the north-west. O'Neill had set off for Kinsale, Co. Cork, to link up with Spanish troops which had landed there on 21ˢᵗ September. From Derry the English and their Irish allies were now free to raid extensively in both the Donegal and Derry area. In November Dowcra raided the Roe Valley. Captain Roger Orme crossed from Greencastle by boat as Dowcra made his way through Cammon Wood, meeting little resistance. Dowcra noted the plentiful wildlife that over-wintered on the shores of the Foyle, wild swans, crane, geese, ducks, teal, plover and seagulls. He was far from being

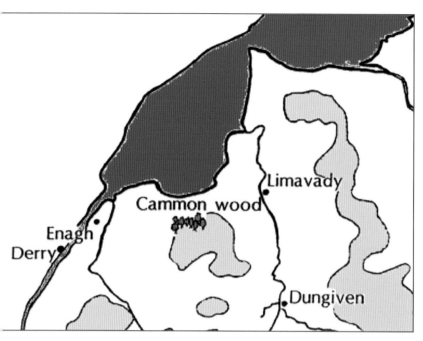

Map showing the location of Cammon Wood

motivated by tourism however as he recorded the great abundance of houses full of corn and butter that he set alight. He took cows, horses, sheep and small cattle, though most of the cows had been driven away before he arrived. Dowcra "wasted" whatever else he found as his soldiers pillaged and looted along the way. The Irish were killed, including farm workers, women and children. By April 1602, Dungiven castle had surrendered without a fight and by July, Donnell O'Cahan was sueing for peace. He surrendered his lands between the Faughan and Lough Foyle to the Crown, getting title for the rest, except the Dungiven area, which was to go to Cowey Ballagh McRichard O'Cahan.

When O'Neill lost at Kinsale, despite Spanish support, his power in Ulster began to weaken. His eventual surrender in 1603 saw Donnell O'Cahan's general situation worsen in the north-west. The new King James VI of Scotland and James I of England, allowed O'Neill to keep his lands in return for obeying English law. Donnell, who was in fact O'Neill's son-in-law, was once again expected to acknowledge O'Neill's overlordship, despite being promised otherwise by Dowcra. Donnell casting aside his wife, would not have helped his relationship with O'Neill. Donnell still remained irritated with the situation and even a knighthood in 1607 does not seem to have softened the blow. Lord Mountjoy, whose successful strategy had defeated O'Neill, and who was in overall charge, wrote to Dowcra explaining that "the security of Ireland" depended on pleasing O'Neill, not O'Cahan. Dowcra's promise to Donnell O'Cahan would have to be overlooked. Besides, wrote Mountjoy:

> *"O'Cahan is but a drunken fellow and so low in character that he does not know when he is well off."*

The Flight of the Earls

O'Neill himself, however, had made many enemies. Among the English officials in Ireland there were those who felt he had been treated too leniently, given the great threat he had posed. When King James summoned both O'Neill and O'Cahan to London to make his judgement on the matter of the overlordship, O'Neill in particular had some reservations about going. In the preceding few years O'Neill had felt his enemies reduce his power in Ulster, and, while he was confident of a favourable outcome, he knew he would be taking a risk by going to London. The next journey he would undertake would not be to London. In September 1607, O'Neill and other leading northern chiefs decided they could not see a future for themselves in Ireland. Along with around 100 followers he boarded a ship at Rathmullan, Lough Swilly, and set sail for Catholic Spain. The Flight of the Earls, as it became known, would be a major turning point in Irish history. Symbolically this act was to mark the end of the Gaelic clans' domination of Ireland and of the Gaelic order that had lasted a thousand years. The Flight of the Earls left the country with no leadership and completely at the mercy of the invaders and their planned Plantation.

With the Flight of the Earls the authorities seemed to become suspicious of Sir Donnell. He went into hiding near Limavady in the winter of 1608 but was arrested and imprisoned in Dublin Castle. Although he was accused of treason he was never tried and he died in the Tower of London, in 1628. His elder son, Rory, was to be arrested and hanged for having a central part in a plan to secure his release. Rory had wanted to seize Coleraine and burn it along with other Ulster towns. Limavady would be burned and Sir Thomas Phillips, who had captured Donnell, would be killed. By taking hostages he intended to bargain for his father's release. However Rory, like his father, if Mountjoy is to be believed, was fond of a drink and seems to have revealed too much of his plan to the wrong person. This led to the arrest of twenty-five people and eventually to Rory's execution along with five other conspirators.

The English Crown seems to have been a little surprised by the departure of the Earls, but soon saw the advantages it yielded. Clearly this would allow the next phase of the conquest to continue much more easily. The campaign had caused a great deal of human suffering. Three years after arriving in the Foyle with his 4,000 infantry and 200 cavalry, Dowcra was left with 1,000 foot and 50 horse. That included what was left of the 2,000 reinforcements he had been given. The Derry garrison lost 5,000 men killed, wounded or deserted. These figures only account for the military casualties and we can only imagine the civilian toll. While the deliberately induced famine and wholesale murder that brought the Nine Years War to an end, left Ulster a wasteland, there was little exceptional in this in the context of the period. Indeed in the north-west, Dowcra found himself slated by some of his critics for being "too lenient."

The end of the war brought a peace of sorts. Apart from the carnage, it had cost the Exchequer two million and led to the debasement of English coinage. King James wanted to minimise any further expenditure and conflict in Ulster in the coming years and the plans he set out for the province took this into account.

Plantation Plans

Sir Arthur Chichester was made Lord Deputy (1604-1616) and put in charge of planning and organising the Plantation of Ulster. The plan would involve the distribution of about four million acres of land. The system used to allocate the land divided people into various groups.

The first of these groups was called 'Undertakers.' These were wealthy men who undertook to bring English and Scottish settlers across to Ulster. This group was allocated 50% of the available land. Based on his experience from earlier efforts, Chichester believed that estates of land needed to be much smaller than before, to be workable. Previously,

Sir Arthur Chichester

large estate owners had struggled to find enough men to come and live on their huge estates. This time estates of 2,000 profitable acres or less would be large enough to attract men of capital who would regard these as an investment. Each would be small enough to allow an Undertaker to fill up the estate with farmers and tradesmen enticed away from his own home area, whether in England or Scotland. The Undertakers were obliged to build fortifications on their land, provide arms in readiness against attack and to ensure their tenants lived near these newly built fortifications. With 1,000 acres the Undertaker would have to build a brick or stone bawn. With 1,500 or 2,000 acres the bawn would have to be of stone and also have a castle. The 'planters' that the Undertakers brought over had to be English, or inland Scottish Protestants and they would be expected to pay £5 6s 8d to the King for every 1,000 acres, in rent. The rules for the Plantation stated that there would have to be twenty-four 'planters' on every 1,000 acres, from at least ten families. The London Guilds, or Companies, who had already been involved in the Plantation of Virginia, formed part of this 'Undertakers' group. Under the scheme they would eventually become important landowners within this category obtaining around 10% of the land.

The second group was called 'Servitors.' These were soldiers or officials who had served the Crown in the Nine Years War. Sir Thomas Phillips, who would play a vital role in the establishment of the town of Limavady, came into the reckoning in this category as a captain who had fought with distinction against O'Neill. While Servitors would have to erect the same fortifications as Undertakers, they were permitted to have Irish tenants on their land.

A third group was composed of those native Irish who had remained loyal to the

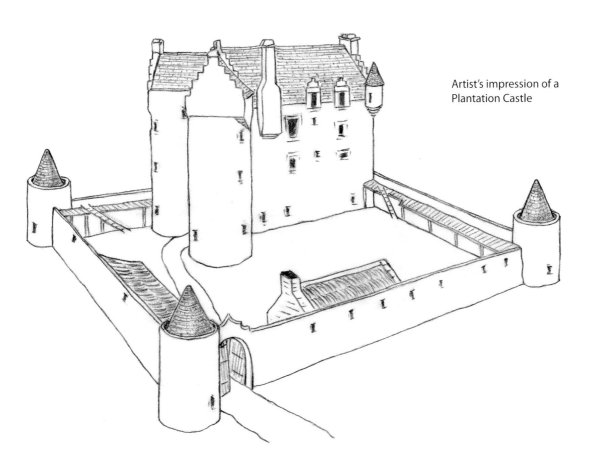

Artist's impression of a Plantation Castle

Crown during the war. These 'Loyal Irish' were allocated around a tenth of the plantation land in the redistribution. They were permitted to have Irish tenants, but were expected to build the same fortifications as Servitors and to use English farming methods. They had to pay £10 13s 4d per 1,000 acres for their land.

The fourth and final group was a mixture of various other bodies. This comprised Trinity College Dublin, six free schools and the Church of Ireland, all of which obtained land in the Plantation.

Private undertakers had already started the Plantation of Antrim and Down and the Plantation of the six counties of Donegal, Fermanagh, Tyrone, Cavan, Armagh and Coleraine got underway in 1609. There was no lack of interest by prospective planters in four of the counties on offer, but Coleraine and part of County Tyrone posed problems. The land between the Bann and the Foyle and Lough Neagh and the River Blackwater had been the Earl of Tyrone's heartland. This was forested and remote and was likely to be crawling with woodkerne, O'Neill's disbanded soldiers. Chichester thought the whole area should be offered to the merchants of the City of London.

In April 1609 Sir Thomas Phillips travelled to London to urge City merchants to 'plant' the county of Coleraine. Phillips had worked energetically developing his lands in Coleraine, but knew they remained exposed. The lowlands were inhabited by the resentful O'Cahans and the settlements were constantly threatened by gangs of woodkerne.

Under-populated and under-developed, Ulster offered prospective colonists a secure title to cheap land, plentiful fisheries and great areas of valuable woodland. There was the chance of a quick return on the investment by converting these woods into barrel staves, ship timber, rafters and charcoal for iron smelting. A great migration to Ulster had begun, drawing people of every class of British society. Soldiers who had fought to conquer the land, like Sir Arthur Chichester, found their friends and neighbours eager to join them in this new venture. Scottish nobles, artisans, evicted Scots farmers, horse thieves and fugitives from justice joined in. While the English had more capital, the Scots, coming mostly from south-west Scotland, Lanark, Renfrew, Stirlingshire and the Borders, were the more determined planters.

Despite all this the London Companies gave a less than enthusiastic response to the plea made by Phillips, that they would join him in the north-west. He made a strong case about how "in the woods 20,000 swine for bacon and pork" could bring an annual profit of £3,000 to £4,000. He told them of the profits possible in oatmeal and oatmeal groats, hide and tallow, beef, butter and cheese. A great deal of Royal pressure was also exerted and eventually, later that year, a number of commissioners travelled to Ulster to map the land and determine who could claim to own what. They landed at Carrickfergus in August 1609 and Phillips himself escorted them from there to Coleraine. From Coleraine Sir Thomas Phillips took them along Lough Foyle to Limavady and on to Derry and Lifford. After spending a few days in Lifford, the agents returned again to Coleraine. The Lord Deputy and Governor General of the Plantation, Sir Arthur Chichester himself, took them from Coleraine to Toome, showing off supplies of iron ore, the good land, the woods and the full extent of the River Bann.

Suitably impressed, the commissioners took 'some of the country's commodities such as salmon, eels, yarn, hides, tallow, iron ore and pipe staves' back to England with them. When the commissioners returned to London, the city merchants agreed to take on the 'plantation' and development of the city and county. With this in mind, 'The Honourable The Irish Society' was set up to look after the Companies' interests. In the centuries to come the London Companies would fund several building projects on the acquired lands. St Columb's Cathedral in Derry and the model farm at Church Hill House in Ballykelly are two notable examples and they also influenced the planning of towns and villages in the area.

The four baronies

Coleraine

Tirkeeran

Keenaght

Loughinsholin

The London Companies' preference was to give greater prominence to the site at Doire at the expense of Coleraine, which lost its county status. The city and county were renamed Londonderry in 1613 and comprised the four baronies of Tirkeeran, Keenaght, Coleraine and Loughinsholin. Twelve London Companies were granted land in the county and this included the O'Cahan lands. The Companies involved in the Limavady region were the Grocers, Haberdashers, Fishmongers and Skinners.

Plantation Settlements

Eglinton

Founded by the Grocers Company in 1619, Eglinton village was originally given the name Muff. The Company leased the area to an Edward Rone and when he died, Robert Harrington, his brother-in-law, completed the lease conditions. This involved building a castle, a bawn and twelve houses. These formed the basis of the village of Muff by 1622, until the later addition of Faughanvale Parish Church in 1626. During the renovation and general renewal of the village that took place in the 19th century, the original church was replaced, in 1821 to be precise, by the present day St Canice's Faughanvale Parish Church. The east gable of the old building still stands though, a picturesque ruin in the graveyard of the new church. As with all the Plantation settlements, Muff saw troubled

The east gable of the original church in the graveyard of St Canice's Faughanvale Parish Church

times in the years that followed its establishment. It suffered in the 1641 Rebellion and from the attentions of King James' troops during the period of the Siege of Derry.

Ballykelly

Ballykelly or Baile Ui Cheallaigh, the homestead of the Kellys, is built on lands granted to the Fishmongers in 1613 by King James I. Allocated 3,210 acres near the Foyle, they established the village and a castle at Walworth. Fragments of this original settlement remain. These include parts of a fortified house and bawn, as well as the ruins of St

Peter's old church at Walworth, built in 1629. Also known as the Garrison Church, this appears to have been the only new church built by the Planters in the Limavady area in the 17th century. The church led a chequered life being destroyed in 1641, restored in 1664, then destroyed again in 1689 and then restored again in 1692, this time by William III. The fortified bawn at Walworth House is of considerable archaeological importance. Though the connecting walls have long since been destroyed, three of the flankers of the original bawn remain in situ as they appeared in the 1600's. The fourth flanker was demolished around 1730, when the present day 'new' Walworth House, was built. The name 'Walworth' came from an estate that the Fishmongers had in Surrey. The name had been used back in 1705 for another house situated near Shackleton Crescent on what was more recently the 'married quarters' of the British Army base. Although the south-west tower of the fortified bawn at the 'new' Walworth is long since gone, the three remaining towers are well preserved and are particularly remarkable because

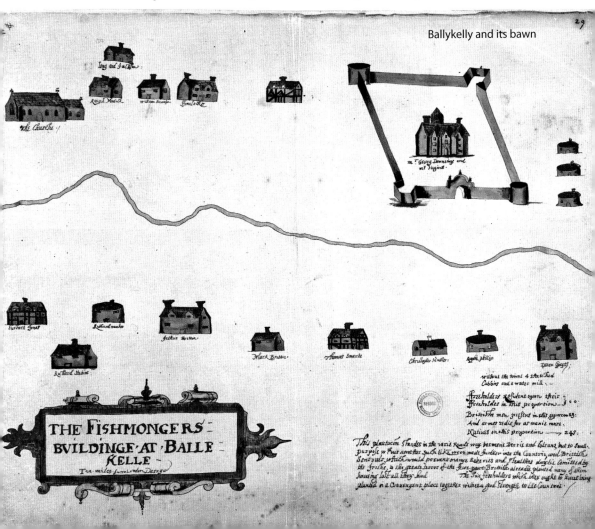

Ballykelly and its bawn

St Peter's Old Church or the Garrison Church, Walworth

of their difference in shape. The south-east tower is perfectly circular with a diameter of eighteen feet and walls three feet thick. The north-west tower on the other hand, is elliptical in shape. The north-east tower is different again and forms a five-sided figure. In time, the Fishmongers' estate would pass by lease to the Hamiltons and the Beresfords before finally being regained by the Fishmongers again in 1820. They reinvested in the village creating much of what remains today.

Sketches of the three remaining flanker towers

Dungiven

In the Dungiven area, Sir Edward Doddington was given the lease of the Skinners Company Estates in the county. This included not only all the land around Dungiven, but also thousands of acres in the Banagher, Ballinascreen and Claudy districts. At Crossalt, or Brackfield as it is now called, Doddington built a bawn which Nicholas Pynnar described for The Honourable Irish Society in 1619 as:

> *"a strong castle of lyme and stone being 40 ft long and 34 ft broad with two turrets to flank it; also a bawn of lyme and stone 100 ft square, 14ft high and 4 flankers. There is also a church adjoining the castle."*

Working hard to protect his estate and to comply with the regulations of Plantation, he added two villages of twelve houses in the vicinity. Though no evidence remains of the villages, substantial ruins of the castle and bawn have survived to this day and can be visited. Brackfield Bawn is situated close to the main road that runs between Dungiven and Londonderry and it is now in the care of the Environment and Heritage Service. At Dungiven itself, after repairing the former O'Cahan castle there, Doddington added a house for his own use and an all important bawn for its protection. Phillips described the house in 1622 as being a two-storey stone built house, forty-six feet long by twenty-one feet broad. The repaired towerhouse was three storeys high, slated and with a round flanker. A sketch from 1611 shows Doddington's fortified enclosure with out-buildings on the side nearest the river, and with the Priory on its other side. The towerhouse can be seen to adjoin both the house and the Priory.

Crossalt Bawn

Sir Edward Doddington's house and bawn at Dungiven in 1611

Doddington also set up the town of Dungiven in line with the plans set out for the Plantation, bringing over mainly Protestant tradesmen with their families to people it. According to a survey by Nicholas Pynnar in 1618, there were twelve houses built and it is reasonable to assume that these were located not far from the present town's Main Street. Doddington died in 1618 and his young widow, Anne (nee Beresford) married Sir Francis Cooke of Desertmartin. She went on to outlive him also, seeing out her days in Dungiven Castle as Lady Cooke. After her death it is known that Careys held the lease in the 1680's and then the Ogilbys, though evidence indicates that the house became derelict for a time and that it had burned down in the 1670's. The restoration work to the Priory meant that Protestants would worship there and no Protestant church would be built in the town immediately.

Much is known about Dungiven following excavations at the Dungiven site carried out by Dr Nick Brannon during the late 1970's and early 1980's. These turned up several hundredweights of ornate ceiling plasterwork. Rosettes, three-dimensional pineapple-shaped pendant bosses, and shallow-relief tulips, fruit and foliage, fleur-de-lys, oak leaves and classical columns were found on the site interspersed with 'ribs' which framed hexagonal and circular panels. Brannon has explained that the various bosses and 'ribs' would have been made beforehand in wooden moulds, while the ceiling would have been assembled 'in situ' by a skilled plasterer. The plasterer would first have applied a course plaster undercoat to wooden ceiling laths. The finer plaster of the decorative ceiling panels would then have been put in place, using a glue of wet lime. The plaster itself comprised sand, clay and calcium carbonate and the moulds needed to complete the work would have been re-used time and again on other work. Ceilings in the style of the one revealed at Dungiven are rare in Ireland in this period and are more in keeping with the large houses and halls found in late Elizabethan England and Wales. Brannon considers it likely that Doddington specially commissioned the ornate ceiling to be placed in the former O'Cahan towerhouse and had it carried out by an experienced English artisan who travelled to Dungiven to complete it. Done to the exacting standards of the day, the ceiling would certainly have impressed visitors to Doddington's home.

Ballycastle

Along the lands of the lower Roe and a short distance from Limavady, sat the Haberdashers' plantation. With a lease of fifty-one years starting around 1616, their first farmer was Sir Robert McClelland. He brought over one hundred and twenty-seven people, including many of his own family, as well as other Scots from Galloway. McClelland built a castle and bawn at Ballycastle, on the site of Aghanloo old church and an earlier Norman castle. About a mile from this castle, near the Curly Burn lay the village of Artikelly which is well illustrated on a map of 1622 as a single street with a few

cottages and Irish cabins. For those who know the area it is tempting to align the present day settlement at Artikelly with that shown on the 1622 map, but as yet, no archaeological evidence exists to substantiate this. McClelland died in 1641 and by 1657 most of the Haberdashers' land was under the control of Randal Beresford.

The Haberdashers were only loosely connected with the scheme though, and from 1611 had transferred their interests to two of its freemen, Adrian Moore and, the aptly named, William Freeman. They did this when it had become clear that the Companies would be expected to contribute to the wider Plantation scheme as well as their footing the costs of improving their own particular portions of it. They began to

McClelland's castle and bawn at Ballycastle, Aghanloo

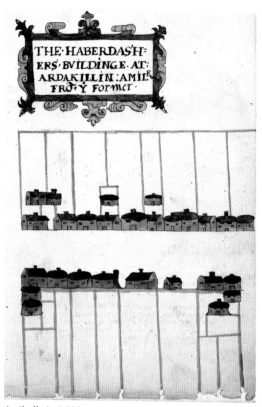

Artikelly in 1622

fear the relentless financial demands being placed on them and set up various leasing agreements. The arrangements proved successful however and when Phillips was surveying the Plantation for the government he cited the Haberdashers' lands as a good example of what was being done properly in the area.

Magilligan

This area was almost exclusively Church land belonging to the See of Derry. One half of the townland of Ballycarton was however leased by the Gage family from Northamptonshire. The Normans had first introduced the harvesting of rabbits in the area in the 13th century as a commercial enterprise and the Gage family were quick to exploit the rabbit population they found in Magilligan. It was a lucrative business with the ready supply of fur very much in demand for lining expensive hats and gloves. By the 1660's the Gage demesne saw fit to employ a warrener to oversee the rabbit warrens on its lands.

Limavady and Sir Thomas Phillips

The area around Limavady, along with land in Bellaghy, was given to Sir Thomas Phillips, a professional soldier who had travelled widely in Europe, learning French and Spanish along the way. Having arrived in Ireland as a captain, Phillips was subsequently knighted at Drogheda on 26th March 1606 for his part in the conquest of Ulster.

He had been given command of the fort at Toome in 1602 and custody of Coleraine Abbey in 1604. A

Sir Thomas Phillips

typical soldier or servitor of the period fighting for the Crown, Phillips could rightly expect to be rewarded. He had married Alice Usher, the daughter of Sir William and Lady Usher, whose grandfather was the Lord Chancellor and Archbishop of Dublin. A former Governor of Londonderry, by 1610, Phillips had obtained a good collection of land and rights in the north-west. He had also become chief advisor to the Crown on the proposed plantation of the county of Londonderry. In the Coleraine area Phillips had acquired fishing rights on the Bann at the Salmon Leap, and permission to hold a weekly market in the town. He got a lease on the ferries

The signature of Sir Thomas Phillips on a document he sent to the King

and customs in the area, and set up a trade in timber with England and Scotland. It was Phillips who, in 1608, obtained the licence for what was to become the oldest licenced distillery in the world, the Bushmills Distillery. No less than 400 years later it is still going strong and we can only dream of what might have been if Phillips had waited another two years to get the licence when he came here to Limavady.

In 1610, on the understanding that he give up his rights in the Coleraine area, Phillips received 3,500 acres in the Roe Valley that centred on Limavady, in addition to 500 acres around Castledawson. He played down the acreage and its worth as the 'horsepond of Limavady' and the 'cabbage patch of Castledawson,' but, by the time he was finished, he was reckoned to have control of about 4% of the entire county. With typical vigour, he soon set about making improvements to his new estate. He extended and repaired the O'Cahan castle and dug out a surrounding ditch. In front of the castle Phillips built a slated two-storey stone house complete with a leaded bay window. He also laid out a formal pleasure garden, an orchard and a dovecot and created a fishpond next to the house. All of this can be clearly seen in the first map of the area drawn by Thomas Raven in 1622 for Phillips, around eleven years after he had begun his renovations. Archaeologists Dr Nick Brannon and Dr Audrey Horning have recently begun to excavate the site. With agricultural buildings and industrial features in evidence on the Raven map it is possible that Phillips may have housed his workforce at the site. While their investigations are still in the early stages, the site remains largely unspoiled and the team is optimistic of being able to locate, reveal and explain much of Phillips' endeavours there. A building on the map with a large chimney suggests Phillips built a

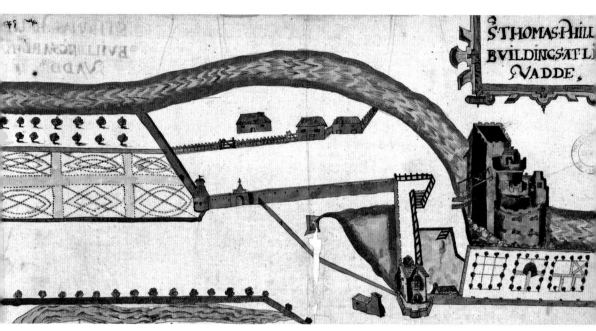

Phillips' castle, house and gardens

'malt house' for brewing beer, which at this time was an important commodity.

The archaeologists believe they may have precisely located his castle at the site, which appears on the map as having a drawbridge, moat, circular tower, and battlements with double tiers of guns. It seems also to have had some of the original Irish settlement clustered around it at this time. A water mill and a mile long mill race were constructed, though this race was more than likely a renovated version of the old race built by the Normans for their mill on the Roe or Roo, as they called it. To make lime for his buildings Phillips had shells brought up from the Foyle and many of these very shells have already been painstakingly uncovered. Defensive walls ring the site and the long, zig-zag fence around its border is preserved in today's field boundary. Some artefacts have been found where there had been some collapse at the river's edge. Fine ceiling plaster work and Venetian glass have been unearthed along with fragments of drinking vessels from the 16th and 17th century. The plasterwork of Phillips' ceiling throws up echoes of the work done at Dungiven around the same time, for Sir Edward Doddington. The Ordnance Survey Memoirs of the 1830's made reference to corniced ceiling work having been part of the interior of Phillips' building and stated that plaster cornices and a 'rib' were uncovered on the site around that time. A connection would scarcely be surprising.

Phillips and Doddington were two former soldiers who had both been knighted for their services to the Crown. They were living within a few miles of each other and had to co-operate, of necessity, if they were to hope to survive in this new Plantation. Indeed we know that Doddington was a burgess of Phillips' 'newtowne' when it was given its charter and there is little doubt that they kept in close contact. With both men renovating similar towerhouses in the same valley around the same time, it is possible, if not even highly likely, that the same plasterer was employed on both sites.

By 1610 Phillips had laid out the village of Newtowne Limavady on its present location, a mile or so down river of the former O'Cahan stronghold. This comprised eighteen small houses arranged around a crossroads with a stone cross in the centre. The village also featured a two-storey English style inn, which Phillips had built for the benefit of those passing through the region. Said to have measured forty-six feet long by seventeen feet broad, the inn can be easily picked out on the map as the building with the large sign hanging out in front of it. As a servitor, Phillips was not required to 'plant' the land. He could have taken Irish tenants who would have had to pay £8 per 1,000 acres, but he populated the town with twenty-five English and Scottish families. They paid a rent of £5 6s 8d. per 1,000 acres and their presence would add much needed

Newtowne Limavady

security. A Monday market was initiated which was to continue in Limavady right up until the 21st century. Though James I had actually signed the charter at Hampton Court on 26th September 1612, the work was given official approval on the 31st March 1613, when the settlement was granted its town's charter.

When Phillips died in 1636 the estates of Limavady and Moyola remained in his family and passed to his eldest son Dudley. Limavady town suffered greatly in subsequent years and we have to use a good deal of imagination along with hard evidence from sources, to be able to piece together what the village of that time would have looked like in reality.

Cagework houses were commonly used. The timber frames for these were sometimes shipped directly from England and assembled here. More often though they were made from timber cut locally. The gaps in the frames were filled with clay and wattle. Plans were set down to guide the layout of these new towns. Each town usually had a central square containing the public buildings such as the town hall, the courthouse, the jail and sometimes the church. From this square the streets ran straight and wide forming a grid pattern. The houses faced onto the street and each had a long garden behind. These houses were generally two-storeys high and built either of timber or of stone with slated

17th century village main street leading to the house and bawn (reconstructed in the former History Park, Omagh)

or occasionally thatched roofs. In some towns the main streets were paved with cobbled stones.

The people living in the towns were normally merchants, shop-keepers or artisans such as smiths, carpenters, and masons. In the 1630's names like Lawson, Jalks, Poke, You, Carradhouse and Gas are recorded around Limavady as well as names that are more familiar to us such as Ross, White, Martin, Boyd, Stephenson, Nicholl, Millar, Conn, Crawford, Moore and Connell. Most of those who lived in towns were English or Scots, as the Irish only gradually became accustomed to town life and they were discouraged, to some degree, from settling in these new towns.

Those Irish who did settle would often have lived in a separate Irish Quarter such as can be traced in Carrickfergus. These new towns were surrounded by a hostile population and were in constant danger of attack. They were well protected by walls of stone or by earthen ramparts. The townsmen had to be armed and able to help defend the town against the enemy. Each town though took into account the local terrain. Finding an easy place to cross the river or build a bridge were important considerations. Limavady's site was no doubt chosen to take advantage of

'Beehive' shaped Irish cabbons/cabins

the raised area on which it sits to this day and the natural protection provided by the River Roe.

While Phillips tried hard to improve the status of the town, it was to remain a village as Coleraine and Londonderry developed. Their development though took place in some ways despite the efforts of the City of London Agents. Phillips was soon in open dispute with the London Agents. By 1612 he had been deprived of his former land and rents for almost two years, since the original handover. Phillips complained regularly about them and in 1617 he accused them of failing in their duties. A survey by Captain Pynnar in 1618/19 revealed the Plantation to be in a perilous state. Only 642 British males were found to be capable of bearing arms in the whole County of Londonderry. Phillips' own survey in 1622 was equally damning. He reported that in the Grocers' proportion, robberies and murders were a daily occurrence. Even in the Haberdashers' estates, which he considered to be the strongest plantation, great losses were being sustained to the ever-present and menacing woodkerne.

Although 875 acres should have been assigned to set up Limavady and Dungiven as corporate towns, this was not done, and only Limavady was eventually to obtain this

An accurate model of Moneymore village as it was in Plantation times

status. A free school should have been set up using 375 acres out of monastery lands, but this was never done. A gaol and Sessions House was authorised for Limavady in 1612, being mid-way between Coleraine and Londonderry, but the London Companies' influence prevented this from happening. Indeed, according to Sir Arthur Chichester, it seems that, apart from their own workmen, the Companies never brought over a single settler. This would of course have serious implications for the security of the entire project.

Around the Roe Valley some of the Irish still held land in scattered areas. The O'Cahans, the O'Mullans and the McGillegans together occupied important territory that surrounded the Roe Valley. In 1624, as overseer of the Plantation in the area, Phillips urged that defences be strengthened and that any native Irish on Company lands be required to take the Oath of Allegiance and Supremacy. In 1627, the dispute between the Crown and the City of London came to a head. The City had clearly failed in its obligations. The entire British male population of County Londonderry in 1627 was 922 compared to 2,474 Irish. That figure excluded the 'idle persons' and the woodkerne skulking in the county's forests. In consequence The City of London and the

Irish Society were found guilty of non-compliance with the Articles of the Plantation and the Guilds were fined £70,000 and lost their charter in 1635. The following year Phillips died at his home in Hammersmith. An astute soldier, he had always warned of the dangers that lay beneath the surface in the county and in the province in general. He saw firsthand the lack of thoroughness being put into carrying out the Plantation on the ground and had long been uneasy with the overall picture. No later than 1628, he had warned the Government that the smouldering discontent of the native Irish could lead to a sudden rising. He predicted, they would rise up and cut the throats of "the poore dispersed British." Now it would be his sons who would confront the reality of this, just a few years later, in 1641.

The 1641 Rebellion

Having inherited the estate around Limavady in 1636, it would not be long before Dudley would have to fight to defend it, just as his father had predicted. Catholic discontent had been building up. Not unexpectedly, Catholics were resentful, not only at having lost their lands, but at then having to pay high rents to live on these very same lands. They were soon further infuriated at having to pay fines to the King for not being members of the Established Church. Even those wealthy Gaelic Irish Earls who had land were having difficulty, simply in trying to adjust to their new lifestyles. Used to being able to extend extravagant hospitality, many led themselves into debt. King Charles' battle for power with Parliament in England, together with a religious revolt in Scotland, presented the Irish with the opportune time and conditions to rebel. It would begin in October, with Dublin Castle being attacked and forcibly taken. While this part of the plan fell at the first hurdle, leaving the Irish inside the castle as prisoners rather than as conquerors, subsequent events could not have gone better. On Friday night 22nd October at 8 p.m., Sir Phelim O'Neill called on Lord Caulfield at Charlemont to invite him to dinner. Once inside the Caulfield's home, however, he seized the fort, imprisoned the garrison and set out for Dungannon.

Settlements at Newry, Lurgan, Moneymore, Down, Portadown, Cavan, Armagh and Fermanagh all fell. Only Enniskillen held out under the command of Sir William Cole. The initial rising was quick and effective, but the Irish Gentry had limited aims: "no harm to the king, nor to the English, nor Scots"- and they needed the support of the peasants.

Within a fortnight they had this support but had lost control of the situation. The peasants had suffered harvest failure, listened to wild rumours and believed in prophecies and they soon became merciless in their attacks on the settlers. Rumour, religion and revenge led them into vicious behaviour. The rebellion was to become notorious for the massacres committed on the Protestant settlers.

Trinity College Library contains thirty manuscript volumes of the sworn statements from survivors. Extracts from these tell, for example, of 12,000 men, women and children being stripped and sent to the mountains and of how only 4,000 made it to Dublin. In the massacre at Portadown, Manus Roe O'Cahan "drowned, shot and knocked on the head" eighty men, women and children. Little mercy was shown and many settlers were burned to death in their houses. Elizabeth Price had "the soles of her feet fried and burnt at the fire, and was scourged and whipped." Tully Castle was set alight and the garrison killed despite the Maguires having promised them mercy.

Portadown Bridge

Movanagher was a vulnerable location for a settlement and a report from a house there encapsulates the scenes that were enacted elsewhere. While John Brown sat by the fire with his wife and his neighbour John Williams, a gang of nine woodkerne burst into his house. After spending the day in the house making "merry with such food and drink as they could find", the kerne then "butchered" all in the house, along with their two "servingmen". Initially around Limavady, Garvagh and Coleraine, there was little change in the circumstances of the settlers. By November though, this had altered. A deposition by a Ballykelly farmer, Peter Gates, says a Ballykelly Papist called James Farrell, at first offered protection to his neighbours. Soon afterwards though, he set upon and murdered Christopher Weeks and his wife, Gabriel Smith and his wife and two children, Sidney Loftus and two of his children, John Carter, John Jameson and various others. There was the usual destruction in the area – corn, cattle and goods taken and houses burned. The Magilligans of Ballycarton, along with Gulduffe Oge O'Mullan of Ballyness, were among those accused of participating in our area. In February 1642 it was said the whole countryside was alight with twenty fires burning at once from Eglinton to Ballykelly, through to Limavady. The castles at Dogleap and Ballycastle had held, although in dire straits. On 21st March 1642, Dudley Phillips and his brother Thomas and others, sent two petitions off to Dublin asking for help. They related examples of the murder and pillage going on and explained that those who had been able to do so, had fled to Londonderry or Coleraine. They estimated that there were about 1,000 men, women and children, with about 300 fighting men, hemmed in at the castles of Limavady and Ballycastle. On one meal a day, they reckoned they could survive for no more than two months, but were finding themselves under attack when going between the castles or when trying to fetch water. Sorties out for food had cost them twenty men but had taken out about one hundred rebels, they believed. They finished their petition by pointing out that they were forced to take more and more risks because of the "women and children, who consume much of our store."

Having themselves lost all in the rebellion, Dudley and Thomas had asked for a commission to command their troops and for money, powder, lead, muskets, pikes and swords. On 4th April their requests were granted and two barrels of powder, forty barrels of herrings and twelve barrels of beef were sent. It would be almost two months, around the 13th May, before the castles were relieved by forces from East Donegal under Sir William and Sir Robert Stewart. On their arrival, the forces found Captain Thomas in charge, with Dudley having gone to Londonderry with three boats to collect provisions. After a night in the castles, the army marched on to relieve Coleraine, via Magilligan. Passing through Limavady on its return, the army was not long out of Limavady when it met with resistance outside Dungiven. On 17th May, two armies met in a full pitched battle which came to be known as the Brack of Gelvin. It is believed that it was fought a quarter of a mile north-east of the main route between Dungiven and Newtowne Limavady, near the Gelvin River. According to Sir William the Irish "had drawn themselves in good order and had the advantage of sun and wind." They had, he said, 3,460 men under the command of various O'Cahan and O'Neill officers, including 300 men under Colonel Shane O'Cahan of Faughanvale and 200 men under Manus Roe of Coleraine. Although Stewart was outnumbered, having only 1,000 men, he had the use of at least eighty musketeers commanded by a Captain Maxwell. The Reverend T.H. Mullin, writing in 1966, says metal artillery balls, seven to ten pounds in weight, "were found in the district many years later by officers of the Ordnance Survey." It was the Irish who lost the day and Manus McCooey Ballagh O'Cahan retreated to Dungiven, where he decided to surrender to Dudley Phillips.

The years 1642-49 were times of great unrest in Ireland. There were four armies roaming the country which were not always under the control of their commanders: the Irish rebel army, the Royalist, the Parliamentary and the Scottish army. Each had a particular self-interest in influencing the Civil War in England, because they knew it would inevitably affect Ireland. Ulster Catholics and Ulster Protestants were each, at various times and for different reasons, opponents and allies of the king. One of the few certainties that could be counted on in the period was that the Protestants and the Catholics of Ulster would almost always remain opposed to each other. By 1646, after taking on and defeating Munro, Owen Roe O'Neill, nephew of the famous Hugh O'Neill, eventually became pre-eminent. O'Neill had been on the continent where he had gained considerable experience fighting with the Spanish Army. At this point, using up-to-date weapons supplied by the Pope, he looked set to take complete control of the situation. Unfortunately for him, the Civil War had ended in England and a talented military commander by the name of Oliver Cromwell was free to sort out the Irish discontent.

Cromwellian Ulster

Cromwell

Cromwell was quickly able to defeat and suppress all comers, giving and expecting no quarter. His time in Ireland began with the siege of Drogheda where he overcame the determined resistance offered by the Royalist garrison, commanded by the English officer Sir Arthur Aston.

The troops were a mixture of English Royalist and Old Irish. When the castle was taken, few inside were spared. Believing himself to be inspired by God in this matter, Cromwell was convinced that by his actions he was simply bringing justice and retribution for the 1641 Rebellion, to "barbarous wretches who had blood on their hands." Wexford suffered a similar fate and as with Drogheda, surrounding towns soon surrendered, quickly understanding what it would mean if they did not do so. By 1652 all Royalist opposition, including that in Scotland, had been crushed. In Ulster the subjugation of the province was led by Colonel Robert Venables on behalf of Cromwell. He would be supported by Sir Charles Coote, the Commander of the Derry garrison. After successes in Newry, Belfast and Lisburn, Carrickfergus fell to Venables and Coote.

Circumstances in Ulster began to favour them further with the death of Owen Roe O'Neill in November. Bishop Herber McMahon of Clogher was then elected to lead Catholic resistance to Cromwell. When he put all of Beresford's men to the sword after besieging Dungiven in the spring of 1650, the colonists in the north-west quickly swung behind Venables. The castle at Ballycastle was also taken at this time. Appointed a Major, Phillips held on safely to his castle at the Dogleap, but at the expense of the town of Limavady itself, which seems to have been burned to the ground.

Sporadic guerrilla fighting would continue in Ulster until 1653 and the province suffered as famine and plague swept the country. Wolves became so commonplace that a bounty was offered for killing them. When the fighting ended, only those landowners who could prove their loyalty were excused punishment. Hundreds were executed, including this time, Sir Phelim O'Neill. Around 12,000 people were transported to various West Indian islands, where they were set to work as slaves in the sugar plantations.

Millions of acres of land were confiscated and 3,400 soldiers were exiled to the

European mainland. Protestants who had been disloyal were generally absolved if they paid a fine, and while some Catholics were compensated with land in Leitrim, landowning Catholics in Ulster became almost non-existent. The Cromwellian period dramatically altered land ownership in Ireland passing it to mainly Protestant hands. The changes in land ownership nationally were reflected locally. In the turmoil since 1641, the town of Limavady had once again suffered and as a result of their participation in the rebellion, several native Irish freeholds were forfeited. These included the large O'Cahan freehold in Bovevagh, the O'Mullan freehold at Ballyness and the Magilligan freehold at Ballycarton.

The situation was tense and number counts were important. The census of 1659 gives seven English and Scots, including Dudley and Thomas Phillips and six Irish, living at the Phillips' Castle. There were seventy English and Scots living in the town of Newtownelimavady, including Thomas Campbell and George Phillips, the grandson of Sir Thomas Phillips, along with forty-six Irish. A few miles away in Ballykelly the settlers were also in the majority. Here there were forty-two English and Scots, including Nicolas Lane, George Downing and Christopher Freeman, compared to thirty Irish. The picture for the whole of the barony of Kennaught was slightly different with there being 1,215 Irish, compared to 1,012 English and Scots.

Out of all the Gaelic landlords in Ulster, only Lord Antrim's lands were restored and by 1688, less than 4% of each of the counties in the province, other than County Antrim, was owned by Catholics. In an attempt to suppress the Catholic religion, around 1,000 priests were banished and anyone caught harbouring a priest was imprisoned. Once more, men who had lost everything, withdrew to the hills and woods, this time to become known as 'tories', an anglicised version of an Irish word meaning 'pursuer' or 'raider.' In the Tandragee area for example, Redmond O'Hanlon's reputation as a 'tory' became so fiercesome that it became a talking point in London. Born in 1640 near Poyntzpass, O'Hanlon had been a Gaelic landowner who had lost everything in the aftermath of Cromwell's settlement. He was eventually betrayed and shot by his foster brother Art O'Hanlon for the benefit of a pardon and the £200 reward.

Life in 17th Century Limavady

Against the backcloth of wider political upheaval, Limavady's Corporation attempted to uphold the rudiments of organised town life, complete with its community rules and regulations. The town had become the focal point for the exchange of goods and produce. Much of the food was grown in the local area. Turf for fuel was cut in the nearby bogs and carted to town for sale. Several different types of craftsmen plied their trade in the town. There were tanners, weavers, coopers and carpenters, masons and thatchers, saddlers and smiths, tailors and shoemakers. In order to be allowed to trade in the town, traders first had to pay a fee to the Corporation to become 'freemen.' This would then allow them to carry on their specific trade. In neighbouring Coleraine not only did the freeman have to pay money, but he was also required to hand over a silver spoon to the Corporation. The son of a freeman was 'born with a silver spoon in his mouth' or in other words, automatically had the rights of a freeman, by birth. Not conforming to the rules could be costly. In 1660, when William Hall was caught breaking Limavady Corporation's regulations, he was fined ten shillings and warned by the Corporation that he was in future only permitted to sell meal and to operate as a butcher.

The special 'Market days' were strictly regulated and the Corporation dictated where the selling of goods could take place. Trading could only commence at 9 a.m. after the ringing of a warning bell. A Town Sergeant was responsible for collecting two pence from

A cooper at work

anyone who opened up the streets when setting up a stall on a Fair day. He would also have been responsible for mending and cleaning the street after the fairs and markets. Cattle, horses, pigs and sheep, Highland tartan, yarn, linen and woollen cloth were sold in Limavady. Wheat, oats, rye, barley, butter and cheese, potatoes, peas and fruit were traded too. Lough Foyle was famous for its oysters in this period and these were sold by the cwt. and half cwt. in the town, alongside fresh fish and barrels of herrings.

A local cooper, such as John Middleton, sworn in as a Freeman on 17th May 1661, would have made the barrels not just for storing the herrings, but for just about everything else from water and ale and wine, to the butter produced on the farms. The province's extensive oak woods were being fully exploited by the new landlords. Leather gloves became very fashionable in the 1600's and if he was fortunate, Robert Thompson, one of the many local tanners, could have cashed in on this lucrative trade. Fine leather gloves or gauntlets were made from the soft skin of stag, kid or goat, and the wealthy men and women of the day were prepared to pay 1s 7d a pair for them. Thompson would have needed a supply of water near to hand and depended on the surrounding countryside for hides and oak bark. He could use the skin of any animal purchased in the market and sold to him by a butcher, such as John Patton, or indeed William Hall who was mentioned earlier. In line with their extensive list of charges, or Docket of Fees, the Corporation would collect one penny for every dozen calf, sheep or goat skins Thompson purchased in this way. He would have found that the oak bark he needed in the tanning process, was readily available locally. There were often reports of trees being stripped of their bark while still standing and many trades depended on the use of wood, directly or indirectly. It would have been Thompson, or one of his fellow tradesmen, who would have supplied the saddler James Hamble and the shoemaker William Henry, with raw materials, for example.

Everyone who owned a horse in the Limavady area would have had to come to the saddler at some point. Hamble would have provided all the harness equipment used on farm and draught horses. Saddles were needed by the local ladies for everyday travel and by the gentlemen of the area such as Peter de la Vie, and William Bentley, both for everyday travel and for going hunting on horseback. Whether intentionally, or unintentionally, the exploitation of the province's forests was not being managed in a way that could allow them to be sustained and renewed. Consequently the time was not that far off when the apparently limitless supply of wood in Ulster was to come to an end.

In 1663 the town appointed an ale taster, Mr Edmund O'Loughery, to test the quality of ale and beer for the Corporation. Later, in 1702, a standard barrel, bushel, peck and gallon were bought to verify standard measures in the town. It seems difficult to imagine O'Loughery's job having to be advertised for very long before it was filled.

Living on the main streets meant householders were required to level the area in front of their own doors with sand and gravel. They were expected to keep the street gutters clean and to take responsibility for cleaning the area in front of their house, as far as the middle of the street. Ditches and lanes had to be kept clear of all general household rubbish and dung, at the risk of prosecution and a fine.

The townspeople's responsibilities even extended to paying one penny each for the repair of the bridge at Ballyclose brook. In order to control disorderly or nagging women, forty shillings was raised to construct a tumbrel or ducking stool, which was installed

A ducking stool

on the Roe bank on the 4th February 1669. This was a chair with straps that could be swung over the river. The nagging or disorderly woman would be strapped into the chair and ducked a few times in the water as a punishment for her crime! While the tumbrel has not survived, the site of the Ducking Stool, on the banks of the Roe between the old bridge and the John Hunter Memorial Grounds, is still known as a local landmark.

At a cost of fifteen shillings to the inhabitants, stocks were also made in 1691. These would be used to deal with other petty crime in the town. Built with heavy timber frames they had holes for feet and sometimes hands so that those who had committed an offence could be left clamped in a sitting position in a prominent place in the centre of the town. Here they were at the mercy of passers-by who might choose to hurl insults, kicks and spits, or rotten food.

A set of stocks from the period

Despite trade restrictions imposed by Westminster on Irish exports of cattle, sheep, pigs, beef, pork, bacon, butter and cheese, economically, Ireland was beginning to progress fairly rapidly. By 1683 Belfast was exporting more butter than any port in Ireland and was soon to become the fourth largest town in Ireland. It had a population of 589 compared to Coleraine's 633 and that of Londonderry with 1,052. There were regularly forty or fifty sailing ships in Belfast harbour with large quantities of corn, butter and beef being exported to France during this period.

Coleraine and Londonderry survived, despite the need for changes in their economy. The two towns had depended heavily on timber in the early years of the Plantation, but now the woods had almost gone and the iron works in the province were in decline due to the shortage of charcoal. The salmon fisheries though continued to be profitable and salted salmon was exported to Venice and Bilbao, with Spain importing 1,885 barrels of salmon from Londonderry alone in 1684. By the 1680's, emigration to Ulster was popular again.

The Plantation then, could be judged a success in many ways, though several of its aims had not been achieved. The colonists clustered thickly in the fertile valleys that the Irish had occupied before their arrival. Inevitably, the Planters and the native Irish intermingled, though in the unique merry-go-round style that fashions politics in the province, Gaelic families dropped the O and Mac to become Protestants, while Protestant planters married local women and became Catholic and Gaelic-speaking in a generation or two. Religion rather than blood would divide the province in the years to come.

James II and William of Orange

On the accession of James II in 1685, despite the growing improvements in the general quality of life in Ireland, religion would again surface to stir resentment, fighting, and war on the island. Ireland was quickly to become a major battleground in a wider European struggle for power.

The new king's actions did little to allay the fears of Protestants in Ireland. In 1685 James appointed Richard Talbot, Earl of Tyrconnell, as his new Lord Deputy. Talbot set about promoting Catholics to all positions of importance in Ireland. Most Privy councillors and judges appointed were Catholics and, other than Donegal, all counties had Catholic sheriffs. New charters gave Catholic majorities to all corporations except Belfast, and the army was purged of Protestant officers. In England, James caused himself more problems than he could handle when he tried to reduce the power of Parliament. While the English nobility were more concerned with preserving their own powers and privileges, William of Orange, the person they turned to for aid, had other motives. William's overriding aims in sailing for England, were to save the Dutch Republic from imminent destruction and to ensure European stability. Two years later, when he landed at Carrickfergus, these would still be his aims.

Even before William and Mary had been crowned, things were happening in Ulster which would come to shape both William's future and indeed that of Europe. For a brief moment, much of the future history of Europe turned on events in Ireland. On the 3rd December 1688 a letter was found in the street in Comber, Co Down. It was addressed to Lord Mount-Alexander and seemed to suggest that a rising on the scale of the 1641 Rebellion was imminent. Whether the letter was genuine or bogus, copies of it circulated around the country. In Garvagh, George Canning received a copy and sent transcripts on to Limavady and Londonderry. As it was being read out in Londonderry by Alderman Tomkins, a messenger arrived from Limavady with a warning from George Phillips, the 56-year-old grandson of Sir Thomas. The warning alerted the city to the immediate arrival of Lord Antrim and his men, who had been ordered to replace the largely Protestant garrison in the city. His mercenary army of Redshanks arrived in Limavady on the 6th December 1688. The ageing Lord Antrim himself came by coach with his wife and family and stayed the night in the town at New Hall, George Phillips' home, at the top of the main street. The next day, Phillips accompanied Lord Antrim in his coach as he made his way to Londonderry. As their coach approached Londonderry, they were informed that they would be refused entry to the walled city. The Siege of Derry, as it is now known, had begun.

Initially, Ezekial Hopkins, Bishop of Londonderry, advised citizens to admit Lord Antrim's troops, but as the Redshanks began to cross the Foyle on the 7th December 1688, the drawbridge and gates at Ferryquay Gate were closed against them by thirteen apprentices who had seized the keys. This galvanised the resistance inside and those Catholics remaining within the walls were expelled. Lord Antrim decided to send Phillips to investigate on his behalf. On arrival inside the city, Phillips contrived to send a message back saying he had been detained against his will and that it would be unsafe for Lord Antrim to attempt to enter. Phillips was given the position of temporary governor of the city. By this stage the city contained a number of his fellow Limavady people, who had fled there in search of refuge.

The fate of the Protestant settlement in Ulster depended on Londonderry's ability to hold out, but there was more than just this at stake. If it fell, then James could use Ireland as a base to launch an assault on England and Louis XIV would also be a lot closer to overrunning Holland. As the siege continued, Protestants from all over the country poured into the city carrying what they could and eventually leaving only Enniskillen as an alternative refuge in the province. In March 1689, James arrived in Ireland with a French army and must have been buoyed by the progress he made. He took Dublin quickly and all of eastern Ulster fell under his control. Although Enniskillen still held out, in March, the Coleraine garrison had been forced to retreat to Londonderry. In addition to a garrison of 7,000 men, there were probably 30,000 Protestants now seeking sanctuary in the city.

On the inside, the besieged inhabitants were becoming less and less inspired by the leadership of their military governor, Lieutenant Colonel Robert Lundy. His decision to order a general withdrawal to the city of the northern garrisons meant that valuable supplies fell to the Jacobites, James' men. In an address to his officers, Lundy seemed to highlight only the weaknesses and the hopelessness of the situation. Whether he was secretly a Jacobite, or was simply incompetent, he seemed increasingly to be the wrong person for the job of commanding the city through this momentous time. He suffered a further blow to his esteem, in the eyes of the citizens, on the 13th April 1689. In support of the siege, some Williamite troops had entrenched on the west bank of the Foyle. When they were routed in an ignominious defeat and their foot soldiers hacked down, despite

The Annual "Burning of Lundy" in Limavady

having five times more men overall, suspicion again turned towards Lundy. Captain Thomas Ash, maintaining a diary of the events recorded that this "caused suspicion that Colonel Lundy was a traitor to our cause."

With the arrival of James at the city walls on 18th April, Lundy's inclination to open negotiations with him showed that he was out of touch with the will of the people inside. The last straw came when he refused the support of two regiments sent out from Liverpool. Adam Murray, a local farmer who had been involved in the earlier fighting, took it upon himself to lead a revolt against Lundy. Major Henry Baker, a professional soldier from Co. Louth and Reverend George Walker, a Church of Ireland rector, were jointly appointed in his place. Both were to provide inspired leadership in the days to come. Lundy was allowed to slip out over the walls disguised as a common soldier carrying a bundle of match. To this day his effigy is burned, as Lundy the traitor, in an annual parade in Derry and Limavady. In fact, though regarded as a traitor to the city, Lundy later went on to serve William III. The siege was to continue without Lundy and lasted 105 days in total before it was dramatically relieved on 28th July 1689. Three ships were involved in the relief of the city, the Mountjoy, the Phoenix and the Jerusalem. The three ships combined successfully to break the boom or barricade that had been stretched across the Foyle at Culmore Fort to prevent access to the city from the sea.

Derry was the last walled city to be built in western Europe and the siege was the last great siege in British history. The fact that the city had not fallen meant William gained the time he needed to organise his campaign fully. It was an important symbol too, and not just for William in his European struggle. The Siege of Derry would provide Protestants in Ulster with a potent source of inspiration for another three centuries, particularly during times when they felt under threat in the province. Retreating from the siege in 1689, Lord Antrim's men burned the town of Limavady. Having survived the siege, George Phillips found himself in a deteriorating financial position and was later imprisoned for debt. He recovered sufficiently from this to be elected M.P. for County Londonderry in August 1695. When he died, some time in the first months of 1697, the family sold the entire manor to William Conolly of Kildare. Conolly had to cover the outstanding debts that went with the estate and after commissioning a survey of the lands, he made a series of improvements. While he did some planting on the estate, it is unlikely he lived much in New Hall, at the top of Limavady's main street. Not only did Conolly have extensive properties elsewhere, but he also had responsibilities in Dublin, where he was Speaker in the Irish House of Commons.

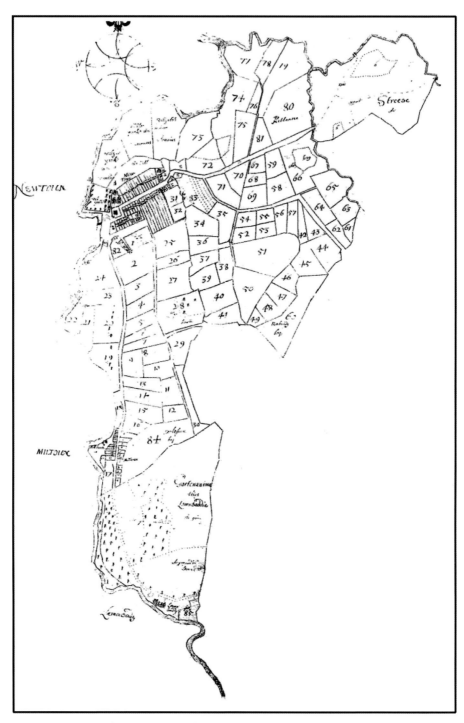

C.R. Phillom's map of Limavady done for William Conolly in 1699

4

Peace, Linen and Revolution – The 18th Century

Catholics, Presbyterians and the Penal Laws

THE TREATY OF LIMERICK, signed on 3rd October 1691, ended the Williamite Wars in Ireland. It set out to be magnanimous towards those who were defeated. Free passage to France to fight for Louis XIV was provided for 1,500 soldiers from Ireland. Those who stayed, and gave allegiance to William and Mary, were to keep their lands and Catholics were to be allowed freedom of worship. William was, however, prevented from fully carrying out his wishes by an Irish Parliament unhappy with such generosity. William did what he could to limit the scope of the land confiscation, but he was a monarch who had been invited to England by Parliament and above all else in the circumstances, the balance of power between Parliament and the King, would have to be respected.

In Ulster, Catholics had little more they could lose. The Earl of Antrim was a notable exception, but in the end he was one of the few who somehow managed to survive and retain his property. Nevertheless, nearly half a million acres of land came on the market. With only Protestants able to buy, prices slumped. William Conolly had been one of those who had ready cash and a good business head. Born the son of a native Irish innkeeper in Ballyshannon, Conolly had become a Protestant and quickly rose to be the richest man in Ireland. The estate he acquired in Limavady, from the Phillips family, formed just a small part of his vast fortune.

The dispossessed had no hope of recovering their lands and were again forced to become tenants of the new proprietors, or to eke out a living as hunted men in the hills. While many Jacobites had taken up the offer to fight in France, becoming known as The Wild Geese, there were still some dispossessed and some discharged soldiers who chose to remain in Ireland and live as outlaws. The southern borderlands of Ulster, that had played host to woodkerne and then to tories, were now the home of the rapparees, so called because of their principal weapon, the half pike or 'rapaire.' While this discouraged settlement in these areas, generally peace returned to most of the rest of the province.

Punitive and severe laws, known as the Penal Laws, were introduced by the Irish Parliament. They would reflect the insecurity felt by the ruling Protestant minority living amongst a population that had made two attempts in the 17th century to wipe them out. These laws prevented Catholics from bearing arms, educating their children and owning a horse worth more than £5. In 1720, Catholics would further lose the right to vote. For a period of time, when William King was Bishop of Derry (1691-1702), Catholics and Dissenters, which included Presbyterians, were persecuted with some fervour. Mass had to be said at night and in remote locations. The Mass Rocks in Terrydremmond and Dunmore were used in this era, as were the Mass Hill at Tartnakelly and the Rough Fort, outside Limavady.

In the longer term, laws brought in to prevent worship, had limited overall success. Pilgrimages continued without interference and priests were allowed to say Mass, provided they registered with the authorities. By 1731 there were twenty-seven priests officiating in the Diocese of Derry. On the Irish Society's lands there seems to have been a good degree of tolerance, with the London Companies building six mass houses at their own expense. A court case brought during the period would substantiate this further. When a local Catholic priest brought a complaint against his congregation for not paying their contribution to his upkeep, the Sheriff of Limavady found for the priest. As the century progressed, the government increasingly neglected the enforcement of religious restrictions. Not only had the Williamite victory of 1690 left Ireland in the hands of a Protestant Ascendancy, but it had also restored the Church of Ireland as the only official church in the country. Supported by state endowment, the Established Church was also entitled to certain taxes or 'tithes,' collected from Catholics and Dissenters. Small wonder then, that the Established Church felt it important to impose and maintain the Penal Laws, not just on Catholics, but on Presbyterians too. Scottish Presbyterians had been making their way into Ulster in numbers even before the Williamite Wars had ended. In the period from 1660 to 1715, this led to a doubling of their existing congregations. The first Presbyterian Church in Ireland was established in Carrickfergus in 1642 by Scottish members of the army that had put down the Rebellion a year earlier. From the beginning of the Commonwealth period, the authorities allowed parishes to pass into the charge of ministers of differing theological backgrounds. From 1655, the Rev. Thomas Fulton ministered to the parish of Newtownlimavady and a year later the Rev. William Crooks ran the parish of Ballykelly. With the restoration of the monarchy in 1660, and the re-establishment of the Episcopalian system, both men were ejected from their parishes in 1661, having refused the option of being re-ordained by bishops.

While not officially able to continue to minister, both were allowed to live on in their districts. As much as these Ulster Presbyterians were seen to threaten the privileges of the Established Church, for their part, the Presbyterians resented having to pay tithes to a Church to which they did not belong. During William's reign their only serious complaint was that their marriages could not be recognised. This in turn presented problems over their rights of succession and for their children's inheritance. However in 1704, a clause in the draft bill to 'Prevent the Further Growth of Popery,' excluded Presbyterians from holding commissions in the army or militia and from being members of municipal corporations. Indeed the view was held by Dr William Tisdall, and shared by no less a man than Jonathan Swift, that Presbyterians were more to be feared than Catholics.

Although an Act of 1719, recognising the educational and religious liberties of Protestant dissenters, heralded the beginnings of religious toleration, it would be 1778 before Catholics were to see an improvement in their legal status. A new spirit of liberalism and tolerance slowly came about when the American War of Independence (1775-83) and the French Revolution (1789) made the English reconsider their views on how best to deal with issues of religion and politics. The draconian attitudes embodied in the Penal Laws were eased.

There were few characters, if any, more suited to the new situation than Frederick Hervey, the colourful Earl of Bristol and Bishop of Derry (1768-1803). In Magilligan, when a new Parish church had been built in Duncrun in 1784 near the ancient Abbey, Hervey gave the old church to the Roman Catholic congregation of the area as their chapel. The building was eventually to prove unsuitable, with a new one, St Aidan's, being built on a nearby site in 1826. The gift was nonetheless a powerful statement of intent by the Bishop and it is claimed that he also allowed mass to be said in the Mussenden Temple, in the grounds of his palace, during this era.

On the edge of the town in 1783, Catholics had built a Chapel at the Roe Mill where a small cluster of houses had grown up near the site of the old Manor mill. This was well in advance of the legal position of the day, since it would not be until the Catholic Relief Bill of 1793 that this would be officially permitted. Even then, this Bill only allowed a Catholic church to be built in a district after an influential Protestant had vouched for the loyalty of the people. Three years later, in 1796, the Beresford family of Walworth would vouch for the Hollow Chapel to be built in Tamlaght Finlagan, Ballykelly. The building was funded by the London Companies and indeed its later replacement would also have received funding, had it agreed to make the move into the village proper. In the wider context, things were clearly changing when the Government's new approach meant that it was happy to establish and endow Maynooth College for the education of Catholic clergy, in 1795. This of course meant that clergy would no longer be enticed to the continent for what was often considered by the government to be a subversive education.

For Presbyterians in Ireland, the restrictions on their creed had not lasted anything like as long. By 1668, they were able to worship openly and began to build simple meeting houses. One was located on the east end of Main Street with another established in the townland of Tullyhoe, Ballykelly. The original church at Bovevagh in Camnish may also date from this period. Presbyterian churches in Limavady, though, generally date from the 18th century. The simple Main Street meeting house would be replaced by a new building, Drumachose Presbyterian Church which was erected on its present site in Church Street in 1743. This 18th century church was then rebuilt in 1875/6, when it took on the 'cross' shape which it retains to this day and which makes it an unusual design as a Presbyterian church.

The London Companies provided assistance for some church building on its lands. Most striking of these, architecturally, is probably Ballykelly Presbyterian Church, designed by Richard Suitor, and built in 1827. A plaque inside the church records the congregation's gratitude to the Fishmongers Company for both their financial generosity and their sense of liberalism.

John Wesley

Following the establishment of a Methodist Society in Londonderry around 1750, this faith eventually spread to Newtownelimavady and a Preaching House was erected in 1773. Although the site of this building is uncertain, it has been suggested it was located near First Limavady Church and Drumachose Presbyterian Church. Later, in 1877, a new purpose-built Methodist Church, designed by Edward McNerlage, was erected in Irish Green Street at a cost of £700.

No less a man than the founder of the Methodist movement, the indefatigable John Wesley himself, had visited the town. Indeed Wesley came to Limavady on four occasions between 1778 and 1789. On his last visit on 3rd June 1789, he was delayed on his journey from Derry when, just fifteen minutes after setting out, the axletree of his chaise snapped in two. Within thirty minutes the preacher, who by this stage was nearing his eighty-sixth birthday, had procured another chaise and was able to continue the three hour journey to Newtownelimavady.

As well as politically enforced hardships, the poor of Ulster were to suffer greatly in other ways in the early decades of the 18th century. Cattle disease and harvest failure caused great distress. When one of Bishop William Nicholson's coach horses was accidentally killed, he was shocked that around fifty people attacked the carcass with choppers and axes to take home food for their families. It was the poorest of the Catholic Irish who would suffer most in these hard times. The English and Scottish planters had come to the province in search of a better life, but when their expectations had not been fulfilled they were ready and able to move on again, even if it involved crossing the Atlantic to reach the New World. In the summer of 1718 an Aghadowey minister led an expedition of five ships that set out from the quay in Londonderry, bound for Boston. When they arrived in New Hampshire these former Ulster settlers named their newest settlement, Londonderry. Catholics had neither the resources nor the inclination to emigrate to these colonies. Between 1725 and 1727 around 3,500 Protestants left Ulster. This raised some concern at the time that the great exodus might weaken the Plantation itself. The search for liberty of religious expression played a role in encouraging Presbyterians to leave, but the difficult living conditions had a vital influence. Rents were virtually doubling in this period which also witnessed repeated harvest failures. By 1729, the exodus had reached its peak, and by 1740, changing conditions meant the population of Ulster was again on the rise.

Limavady in the 18th Century

In 1708, Dr Thomas Molyneux described Limavady as a "very clean English-like town." Access to the town was another issue. Travelling to Limavady from Coleraine on what is now the Murderhole/Windyhill Road, Molyneux praised the "art and industry" of the road's construction. He also remarked however, that the causeway was only partly finished, and that the journey took him four hours over "dismal, wild, boggy mountains." The Corporation Records for the town give sporadic glimpses of life in the 18th century in Limavady.

When the town's Stocks needed replaced again in 1715, it was decided that a levy of 16s 3d would be raised from the inhabitants 'for making a sufficient pair of Stocks.' The following year, in 1716, the Corporation decided to fine anyone leaving anything lying around in the streets at night that might be a nuisance to the public, such as wheel cars, casks or kettles. The fine would be 3s 4d for this offence. While there was no understanding of the relationship between insanitary living conditions and disease, there was nevertheless an underlying desire to keep the streets and the water courses clean.

Householders were given notice not to 'clean' grain on the street, nor even in their own entries, when the wind was blowing 'away' from the street. They were responsible for clearing dung and dirt from opposite their own house and keeping the gutters clean. Indeed, in 1722, householders were ordered to pave the gutters in front of their own doors. In the following year, 1723, a charge of fourteen shillings was levied by the Corporation 'for repairing the Town Well' and it was also decided to fine anyone who left their barrels, or vessels, or hogsheads, at the well. Those who were creating a dam on the Ballyclose brook, and putting their flax in it, were also to be fined. Water was always a major preoccupation and in 1738 we learn that a man was appointed to take care of the local weirs. At this stage, the supply of water for the town came in an open ditch from Tubberin spring and the population of the town in 1764 is recorded as being 2,500 persons. At a public meeting on 19th June 1783, it was decided to appoint a nine man committee to investigate and calculate the cost of supplying water pipes and pumps in the principal street. It was subsequently calculated that the cost would be one shilling per foot and that this should be met by a tax of seven pence per foot on the length of each dwellinghouse and yard entry. Beyond the town's principal street however, the water supply would still come via an open ditch.

Several inns operated in Limavady in the period. In 1766, John Ross advertised the renamed 'Man of War,' as being under new management. Formerly owned by John Mullan, it was claimed that the inn was now fitted up 'in a proper manner for the accommodation of gentlemen who travel the road.' Serving the best wines and liquors there was also good stabling, hay and oats for the horses, complete with good attendants. In 1791, Thomas and William Smith offered an extensive assortment of the best wines and spirits in their inn, which had the added convenience for the traveller of an excellent Post-Chaise and horses, with a careful driver. They gave notice that they could sell spirits by the gallon and wine by the dozen and made it clear too that their grocery and hardware business would continue as usual. On Friday 13th May that year, a cockpit was set up in another inn, David Blair's, for a cock fight which, it was proposed, would commence at 9 a.m. and end at 5 p.m. There was obviously a continued demand for 'accommodation' which William Ross of the Market House sought to capitalise on. In January 1794 he got a lease to build a good room, adjoining his inn, which would be for the accommodation of ladies and gentlemen. We have some idea of what these ladies and gentlemen, and those who lived in the area, were reading at the time. In 1750 the Limavady merchant, Hugh Sherrerd, ordered fifteen sets of Thomas Stackhouse's three-volume 'History of the New Testament.' With no dedicated bookseller in town it was Sherrerd again who ordered the popular 'Dialogues Concerning Education' two years later. Evidence suggests that there were many people who could read a connected narrative in the era. Chapmen, or hawkers, criss-crossed the countryside, selling anything that was cheap, and this included books. It was these chapmen who supplied the general population. They sold to people who had a limited income, but were literate and interested in reading, even if it was not anything too sophisticated or learned.

Linen in the Roe Valley

A major factor in turning around the dire economic crisis in Ulster had been the development of a new industry, linen production. On the invitation of William III, Samuel-Louis Crommelin came to Ireland in 1698 to become 'Overseer' of the Royal Linen industry in Ireland.

A Huguenot refugee from French religious persecution, he was to transform the manufacture of linen here. He devised a means of harnessing water to bleach and weave linen and quickly turned the cottage industry into a mechanised one. Crommelin was operating initially around Lisburn, in the Lagan Valley, but bleach greens were soon being set up on the banks of the tributaries of the Bann.

Samuel-Louis Crommelin

In the 1750's in and John Smith had set Tamlaghtmore and George one at Duncrun. Meanwhile, Roe, the Smith family were Using a mill lead taken from constructed a bleach green and from 1769 leased out wheel, to a Robert Campbell industry was to thrive in the

Magilligan, Henry Lurting up small bleach greens at Lane had started a larger on the east bank of the developing linen bleaching. the Carrick Rocks, they had with three water wheels another green, with a water for thirty-one years. The Roe Valley with fourteen bleach greens in operation by 1782. John Smith of Tamlaght began trading as a linen draper in the area and John Alexander and John Moody had set up as linen merchants. Other wealthy and renowned families like the Ogilbys and McCauslands were involved. The building of an elegant Linen Hall, on the same plan as that built in Derry, was proposed by Marcus McCausland in 1771 and afterwards built in Linenhall Street.

On his death in 1777, Alexander Ogilby was referred to as having been an eminent bleacher and linen draper. The county was the fourth largest producer of linen in Ireland in 1770 and the brown linen sales for the year give an indication of the importance of linen to the Roe Valley at this point. In 1783 for example, Dungiven had sales of £3,100, which compares favourably with Coleraine's sales of £3,900. Limavady had sales of £15,600 that year. Though this is small compared to the figure of £52,000 for Derry and the staggering £130,000 in Lurgan, where the highest sales were recorded, clearly linen played an important role in the economic life of Limavady and indeed Dungiven. On the back of this industry, other related businesses would have developed, similar to George R. Sherrard's starch factory, set up in 1816 in Limavady. The remains of the industry are everywhere in the present day Country Park. The leads that supplied and controlled the water, the scutch mills, the weaving shed, the beetling shed and the greens where the linen was bleached are easily found. In the cottage industry, bleaching was done by putting the woven linen into pots containing buttermilk, potash and other ingredients, and boiling it over a turf fire. The cloth was then rinsed in clean cold water and then stretched out in the sun, on the greens or grassy fields. This had to be repeated about twelve times before the cloth turned white. Bleaching generally took place during April or September and it was a long and awkward process before the introduction of chemical bleaching.

Chlorine and oil of vitriol were used in the industrialised bleaching process before the cloth was stretched in long strips on the bleach green. Watchmen were employed to guard the linen as it bleached. They were provided with tiny stone-built huts which overlooked the fields. The huts were usually circular or square in shape and the work was all the more vital in an Ulster which often had no fences and gates. Apart from the risk of theft, there was the danger that animals could wander onto the linen and trample it. Two fine examples of watchtowers are in situ in the Country Park overlooking a former bleach green.

In Belfast, in 1803, the story of Catherine Devlin, alias Dillon, shows the punishment a thief could face. Found guilty of robbing the bleach green at Drumbeg, the judge ordered that she be hanged. When a petition was presented, showing that the linen she had stolen was worth only four shillings, the judge changed the sentence to 'transportation.'

The Watchman's Hut in the Roe Valley Country Park

For receiving stolen cloth, a James Boyd was given three months jail and placed in the Belfast pillory three times. With little law enforcement there were all sorts of dangers to face for those involved in the linen trade. Towards the end of 18th century, some merchants had begun to specialise in the task of whitening the cloth. This required them to travel the country buying brown linen in the many market towns across the province, such as Limavady. For their own security, these merchants, or their agents, had to go to the extent of organising themselves into small groups, in order to be able to transport the valuable raw material with least risk.

Several traces of this important industry still linger throughout our area. The road into the Park was formerly known as the Green Lane and the Brochan House at the entrance to the Park was once a pin house, making pins for the linen industry, though later it would also serve as a distribution point for food in the Famine. Linenhall Street indeed, in the town centre, owes its name to its connection with the industry, betraying the important place the linen trade once held in the town's economy.

At one time, in the Drumsurn area, there were seven flax scutching mills supporting

A Dungiven street sign records the site of the Bleach Green nearby

the local linen industry. Scutching came early in the linen process and involved taking the woody stalk of the flax plant away from the long linen fibres. Quite apart from the noise and dust in such buildings, working at these unguarded water-driven machines was a dangerous job which could cost a worker a hand, an arm, or indeed his life. The Country Park contains the remains of a Scutch Mill and Loughery's Mill near Drumsurn, which fell into disuse after the Second World War, still has its mill dam, a water wheel and some of its original machinery. Close to Loughery's Mill, five cottages were built for the scutchers, who were allowed to keep the flax stalks known as 'shouse' to burn in their fires. Unfortunately, the five cottages were subsequently destroyed in a late night fire which started when the thatched roof of one of the cottages caught alight.

By the end of the 1700's, four bleach greens are known to have been operating in the Dungiven area. James Boyle owned the Cashel mill and bleachworks, built in the 1780's, and in 1800 the King family owned bleachgreens at Bleachgreen Lane Walk near the Priory. Robert Ogilby, who became the landlord of the Skinners Estate itself in 1794, was a wealthy linen merchant who had made his fortune exporting linen cloth from Dublin. In Dungiven, as in any linen area, the local population would have been able to add substantially to their income by spinning linen yarn in the winter months. The good times that the industry brought would not continue for much longer however. When the eventual decline of the linen industry began to be felt around Limavady in 1835, it was attributed to the unusually low price of cottons and the use of machinery. The introduction of power loom weaving, principally in Belfast in the middle of the century, was a hard blow to the many hand loom spinners who supplemented their income working from their own home. In the county generally, the poor state of the linen industry was to become the most important factor in encouraging emigration. Gradually the various processes were being mechanised. Spinning and weaving machines, first invented for the cotton industry in the North of England, were soon adapted for use with linen. The invention of the steam engine meant coal became the driving force in the industry rather than water. Industries moved away from the inland valleys to ports like Belfast and Derry where coal was easily imported. Flax continued to be grown and steam powered factories were now being established, but in the Roe Valley generally, the widespread and large-scale production of linen was over by the 1830's.

Nevertheless, as late as 1867, coarse linen and fine damask were still being produced in Limavady by the Limavady Spinning and Weaving Company. The company had been set up in 1865 with capital of £15,000, divided into 600 shares of £25 each. Its directors were John Lowry of Whiteabbey, Sir F.W. Heygate of Bellarena and Michael King of Dungiven, along with S.M. Alexander, John Alexander and William Cather of Limavady. The new factory, built opposite the

The original Alexander Terrace with the factory in the background

town gasworks on land leased from John Alexander, was capable of holding 150 steam-driven looms. Some time later, after passing through a recession, the factory was bought by S. M. Alexander who ran it from 1875 until 1886. Subsequently it was sold to the Waterpower Linen Company of Cookstown which ran it until 1926. During The First World War, aeroplane cloth, used in the lightweight planes of the era, was produced in the building. The factory continued working until 1933, having been acquired by Edwin Stevenson and Company of Belfast. The 'Alexander Road' housing development replaced a row of houses known as Alexander Terrace that were adjacent to the factory.

Other Industries

While linen was the catalyst for economic recovery, the north-west only made up 15% of the annual total of brown linen sales in the north. Farming remained the most important activity, but in areas like Magilligan, where this could be difficult on the sandy headland, other ways had to be found to supplement incomes. Here, the sand dunes and marram grass were home to what had become the most extensive rabbit warrens in Ulster. The people of Magilligan were long used to exploiting this for their personal benefit. Trapping the rabbits, with ferrets and nets, they sold the carcasses locally for about 4d each.

Alternatively they ate the meat themselves and sold the skins which found their way to the hatting trade in Dublin. This enterprise had proved so lucrative over the years that the Gage family, who owned the lease of the land, were able to implement a restricted killing season and triple the rents on their land in the 1750's, to 120 dozen rabbit skins. By the beginning of the 1800's, around 2,500 dozen rabbits were being sold each year at 13 shillings a dozen, with up to 40,000 pelts a year being 'harvested.' A rare long-haired variety from Holland was introduced especially to supply the demanding hatters of Dublin in the 1800's, while the meat from a Magilligan rabbit was much prized on the best tables in Belfast. Small wonder the locals honoured the humble rabbit with a prayer known as the 'Magilligan Grace':

> *For rabbits hot and rabbits cold,*
> *For rabbits young and rabbits old,*
> *For rabbits tender and rabbits tough,*
> *We thank the Lord, we've had enough.*

For some, it was perhaps too readily available when in season. The Ordnance Survey Memoirs recorded that farmers' wives often sickened their servants by feeding them rabbit too often. As a result many farm labourers stipulated before hire, that they should not be 'entirely fed upon' rabbit throughout the season, which ran from October to February.

The Lough shore area was still an important source of food and income. The Irish were never very willing to eat fish, except on fast days and the need to eat shellfish was seen as a sign of extreme poverty. The Planters, though, prized the oysters and in times of poor harvests, the produce available from the coastal and inland waters, was capable of saving people from starvation. Oysters from Lough Foyle were famous, while in the months of October, November and December, barnacle geese were trapped in nets on long poles as they flew low over the southern shore.

The great variety of flowers still found in the locality was considered to be the reason behind Tircreven honey fetching the highest price of any honey sold on the Dublin market. Some farmers were even able to pay part of their rent in honey. The fact that goats browsed on the wild thyme and other herbs in the area was credited with giving the goats' whey from Magilligan, a quality above any other in the country. In time, the region began attracting summer visitors in search of the health benefits to be found there.

Whiskey production had long been part of the economy in the north-west. Coleraine was second in importance only to Dublin in the period and nearly all the barley grown locally went to the forty or so registered distillers in the county. When excise duty was hiked in 1799 to increase government revenue, it hit the industry hard. Nevertheless, around Magilligan and on the opposite side of the Lough in the Innishowen Peninsula, the illegal making of poteen continued to flourish. The Ordnance Survey Memoirs of 1835 reckoned that there would have been around 400 illicit stills on the go in the Magilligan area alone at that time.

As it has often done through the ages, the Lough was host to an illegal trade, which at this stage was in whiskey. Barley prices tripled as a side effect of this illegal trade, and landlords, quietly aware of the trade, cashed in, by raising rents.

Denis O' Hampsey

Denis O' Hampsey, who lived most of his very long life in Magilligan, attributed his longevity to 'sober' habits and a diet of 'chiefly potatoes.' Born in Craigmore, near Garvagh in 1695, Denis O'Hampsey moved to Magilligan in his infancy when his father inherited land in the Tircreven area, but was to become a celebrity known well beyond the locality. Blinded by smallpox at the age of three, he began to learn the harp under the tutelage of Bridget O'Cahan. Later, the blind itinerant harper John Garragher, taught O'Hampsey and subsequently he learned his music from two Connaught men, Loughlin Fanning and Patrick Connor. When he was eighteen, O'Hampsey was bought a harp by Councillor George Canning of Garvagh, Squire Gage and a Dr Bacon. This was to be the harp that he would retain all of his exceptionally long life. This very instrument can still be seen to-day in the Guinness Storehouse museum in Dublin. The harp was constructed in 1702 by Cormac Kelly, a famous craftsman of the day from Ballinascreen in South Derry. The inscription on the right-hand side of the instrument alludes to the ancient bog oak used to make it.

> *In the time of Noah I was green,*
> *After the flood I have not been seen*
> *Until seventeen hundred and two I was found,*
> *By Cormac Kelly underground.*
> *He raised me up to that degree,*
> *Queen of music they may call me.*

With this elegant harp O'Hampsey was to become an itinerant musician from around 1713 on. His skill and wide knowledge of music were to give him access to many of the prominent figures of the time. Harpers were much sought after in the homes of the wealthy and O'Hampsey travelled extensively throughout Ireland and Scotland, despite his handicap. During his travels in Scotland, he played for Bonnie Prince Charlie in Edinburgh, in 1745.

O'Hampsey came to even wider prominence following his participation in the Harp Festival of 1792 in Belfast. The Festival was designed to revive and perpetuate the ancient music, poetry and oral traditions of

A drawing of Denis O'Hampsey aged 100 years

Ireland, and in addition, offered the opportunity of financial reward to the participants. There were ten harpers involved in the Festival which took place on the 10th July 1792. Rose Mooney, aged fifty-two and blind, and the only female, had come from County Meath to attend. Others had come from Mayo and Leitrim. With the average age of the group being fifty-eight, William Carr aged fifteen from County Armagh, was by far the youngest. O'Hampsey, who was ninety-seven years old at the time, did not win the first prize of ten guineas. This went to Charles Fanning of County Cavan.

Edward Bunting

He did however, catch the attention of Edward Bunting, the organist at the new parish church of St Anne's, who was employed, along with two other musicians, to take down the 'airs' played at the festival.

Bunting felt Fanning was not necessarily the best performer, but acknowledged that his rendition of 'The Coolin,' with modern variations, had proved popular. Bunting was to be inspired by the music he heard and was particularly taken by O'Hampsey's intricate and unique playing style. Immediately after the festival Bunting set out on a quest to collect the traditional airs of Ireland, starting with a visit to Magilligan to see O'Hampsey. Here, he found that the old harper had an astonishing repertoire that spanned the 16th to the 18th centuries.

By this stage, Denis was living in a cottage near Woodtown in the townland of Ballymaclary. When Frederick Hervey, the Earl Bishop, came to take up residence in the neighbouring Downhill Palace, he became an important and influential patron of O'Hampsey's.

Indeed it was the Earl Bishop who gave him three guineas, and the land rent-free, on which to build his cottage. Denis had married in 1781, aged eighty-six, to a Donegal woman from across the Foyle in Innishowen. She is said to have been much younger than he was and in discussion with the Reverend G.V. Sampson, Denis commented that "it must have been the devil that buckled us together,

O'Hampsey's grave

she being lame and I being blind." Not only was he blind, but he also had a protruding tumour on the back of his head which led some people at the time to refer to him as the man with two heads. Denis O'Hampsey is believed to have died on either the 5th or 11th of November 1807, at the age of 112 years. We are fortunate, no doubt in part because of his great celebrity, that we have been left with many of the details of both his life and music. The great revival of the harp largely coincided with O'Hampsey's life and interest in it waned with his passing. In the 21st century, the Hampsey School of Harpers in Garvagh continue the ancient tradition he practiced, and locally, he is remembered in a memorial stone placed over his grave in the cemetery at St Aidan's Chapel in Magilligan. An annual commemoration event promoting the harp is held in Limavady on or around the 10th November each year and in 2007, the bi-centenary of his death was marked with a concert by the world famous harpist Siobhan Armstrong in the Ritter Rooms, in the Roe Valley Country Park. Famous not only as a harpist, Siobhan Armstrong also founded the Historical Harp Society of Ireland in 2002. The Society commissioned David Kortier of Minnesota to make a copy of O'Hampsey's Downhill Harp and accurate copies are now made available for students to purchase via the Society's website. A bi-centenary commemoration concert was also held in Dundee, in the Wighton Heritage Centre organised by Simon Chadwick, an expert in early Irish and Scottish harp and its music. Armstrong, Chadwick and another renowned and

Seamus O'Kane
with his replica of
the Downhill Harp

gifted harpist, Ann Heymann, are very much concerned with keeping O'Hampsey's heritage alive for modern audiences. On a C.D. released by Ann Heymann she plays a replica Downhill Harp and features two tunes O'Hampsey is known to have played. Rather fittingly, the most authentic copy of the Downhill Harp in existence was made by Seamus O'Kane, a local man from Lower Drum Road, Dungiven. Highly detailed research by an expert in the field, Michael Billings, was undertaken in preparation for the making of the replica. A sample of the wood, taken from the actual harp in the Guinness Museum, showed it to have been made of alder. The replica Downhill Harp made by Seamus O'Kane, is thought to be as close as it is possible to get to the original instrument that O'Hampsey played. It looks and sounds beautiful, and we are fortunate that the harp has found its way to the borough.

Duncrun Cottier's House

Margaret Clyde's cottier's house, from Duncrun in Upper Magilligan, was the very first outdoor exhibit removed to the Ulster Folk and Transport Museum. Occupied until about 1952 by Miss Clyde, at least three generations of her family had lived in the house. Cottiers became an important class numerically in the 18th century, although a few existed earlier than this on some north Derry estates. These were people who rented less than five acres, but more usually, from half an acre, to one and a half acres. They were mainly farm labourers who lived in quite miserable conditions.

Margaret's house was sited close to an old clustered clachan settlement in Magilligan, which suggests that it had very early origins. It would have housed a family who lived by providing whatever services and work they could to the local farmers. The only land attached to the house was the potato garden at the rear, though they probably had a couple of potato ridges on a local farmer's land as well as grazing for a cow.

Originally the house probably consisted of a single large room, but this was later divided into a kitchen and bedroom by a wall which was not actually bonded into the side walls. The floors of the house were earth and while some sods are found in the walls, in general, the walls are built of stone. Sods are used too, in the hearth gable and at the top of the rear wall of the bedroom. A typical feature of this style of peasant house in the north and west of Ireland is the out-shot for the bed, placed on the opposite side from the door and near the hearth. Similar features have been found in Highland Scotland and in the Hebrides. The rounded roof ridge, and the roped thatch, which in this case is

Margaret Clyde's Duncrun cottier's house

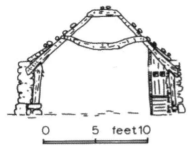

0   5   feet 10

The cruck truss

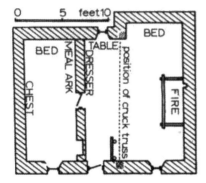

0   5   feet 10

BED   MEAL ARK   TABLE DRESSER   position of cruck truss   BED

CHEST   FIRE

Above: Margaret Clyde's house in its original location

Left: Plan of the house

made of marram grass or bent pulled from the Magilligan sandhills, are features found typically along the coasts of northern and western Ireland.

Of particular interest in the house is the way in which the roof was constructed. Here, an under-thatch of sods is carried by light branches supported by the roof truss. This, it seems, was more a reference to a past tradition of building, than something which was strictly necessary. The same is true of the cruck truss system used in the construction of the roof itself. The principal roof members are fixed to upright posts instead of being rested on the tops of the front and rear walls. While this was normally used to relieve the walls of much of the weight and thrust of the roof, a cruck truss was not needed in a stone building like this one. Again, it is considered to have been merely a stylistic reference to the older traditional building methods. The furnishings in Margaret's house in the Ulster Folk Museum are simple, but suggest a reasonable standard of living for the time. The focus of the house was always the fire, but the furniture was often ready to be pushed back against the walls, as her home was a well-known meeting place in the area for ceilidhing and card playing.

Roe Park House

Around the same time, but at the other end of the social scale, and within sight of

Limavady town, Roe Park House was being built. The land on which it sits was originally the property of the Phillips family, until William Conolly purchased their estate at the end of the 17th century. The house was built in the early 1700's, but there is uncertainty as to whether it was built by William Conolly, or by a Captain Richard Babington.

Roe Park House before its renovation

Portions of the original house still form part of the present day Radisson Roe Park Hotel. The house and demesne were both known as Mullagh until 1743, when Marcus McCausland, whose brother owned Drenagh, bought the estate and renamed the house, Daisy Hill.

Marcus and in turn his son Dominick, made alterations to the house before it was sold to a John Cromie from Portstewart in 1817. It was John Cromie who gave it the name Roe Park. After being sold and resold, the house eventually passed to J.E. Ritter and his wife, the couple who were to introduce hydro-electricity to Limavady in the 1890's. The house's imposing stable yard, with its main block of seven bays, is where J.E. Ritter began his experiments with hydro-electric power. The main wing of the stable yard block has been thoughtfully restored and enlarged and now houses the Coach House Restaurant, as well as changing rooms for the hotel's golf facilities. After Ritter's time, the house was used as an Old People's Home before the Radisson Hotel group renovated and transformed it, adding a swimming pool, gym and accommodation wings that have more than doubled it in size.

Downhill Palace

While the grandeur of Roe Park House dwarfed the humble Duncrun cottier's house in Magilligan, the excess lavished on Downhill Palace, would have been beyond the means of any but a few in Ulster in the period. The long peace that took hold in the latter half of the 18th century allowed the gentry to consider building their homes with beauty and comfort in mind, leaving behind the earlier priorities of defence, safety and protection. This was the era of the 'Great House' in Ulster and there were few, if any, better examples of the extravagance of the age than Downhill Palace built by the

The Mussenden Temple

Earl Bishop, Frederick Augustus Hervey. Choosing the newly fashionable 'wild romantic' style, he adorned the cliff top above Downhill strand with a huge, rather severe-looking palace, which cost him a staggering £80,000. The demesne included the picturesque Mussenden Temple, which has now become an iconic symbol of the area.

Some gentlemen of the time were not overly impressed by the work. In 1801 Justice Day described the Palace as a "sad monument of human folly" and nothing more than a "pile of Grecian Architecture." Eleven years later an Edward Wakefield wrote that he had "never seen so bad a house occupy as much ground." By that stage the Earl Bishop had left Ireland, having set off in 1791, to travel around Europe collecting art treasures. He was arrested by none other than Napoleon though, and accused of spying. The Earl spent nine months imprisoned in Milan and the art he had collected was confiscated. He himself reckoned this to have been £18,000 to £20,000 worth of art treasures. Perhaps there was a good side to this in that it meant the treasures would be saved from the fire that was to destroy Downhill in 1851. The Earl Bishop nevertheless lost an impressive collection in the fire, including paintings by Rubens, Dürer, Correggio, Tintoreto and Murillo. Having long since had its roof dismantled, the former Palace is now a ruin that generally seems to attract less attention than the fully restored Mussenden Temple, which now hosts a variety of functions throughout the year, from weddings to classical music concerts.

Streeve Hill House

Streeve Hill House was originally the home of the Gage family. The estate adjoined Fruithill and has since been incorporated into the Demesne of Drenagh. According to the O.S. Memoirs, it was built around 1735 and at one point was used as a residence for two families, possibly the Robinsons and the Hemphills, before being altered in the 1800's. As it stands today, it is one of the best examples in the area of an early 18th century house. Sensitively restored in 1967/8, an upper floor of the house has been replaced. It seems that this floor was previously removed from the original, supposedly because it interfered with the view from Drenagh. The well-appointed house now operates as a Guest House within the Estate.

Cushy Glenn

In the 17th and early 18th centuries, travelling between Limavady and Coleraine on the old mountain road could be a very treacherous business.

Several travellers simply disappeared, falling victim to the many highwaymen and robbers operating between the two towns. The desolate and eerie road seems to have been a favoured place to waylay people even from as far back as the 1600's when Black Hugh O'Cahan preyed on passers-by. Later, in the 1700's, Roddy Dempsey, Rory Roe O'Harron, James Swann and Joseph Scott terrorised travellers along the route. In the wider region even government forces were not immune to attack. General Napier and his men were ambushed at General's Bridge in Feeny by the infamous highwayman Shane Crossagh O'Mullan. Robbed of their valuables they were forced to walk naked from there to Derry. It was however to be one of his last acts. In 1722, O'Mullan was hunted down and hanged in the Diamond, in Derry. He is buried in the grounds of Banagher Church.

By far the most notorious highwayman in the Limavady area though, was the infamous Cushy Glenn. Cushy was sometimes known as Paddy Cushy Glenn in order to distinguish him from his brother James Cushy Glenn who was executed in Derry for stealing three bullocks from a Mr Hughy. Despite the fact that he was operating in the late 18th and early 19th centuries, the legend of Paddy Cushy Glenn has survived to this day. Cushy was famed for attacking travellers on the top of the mountain, near the former Ram's Head Inn, and dumping their bodies a short distance away. Cushy was eventually to meet his death in 1806 at the hands of a young cloth merchant called William Hopkins, from nearby Bolea. Cushy Glenn's tactics were straightforward. He hung about the inns in Coleraine or Limavady, or wandered around the towns on 'fair' days, looking for people who might later be travelling the mountain road alone. He would then ambush, kill and rob his victim. Born in Magilligan, Cushy is said to have spent some time in the army, where he learned how to handle weapons and how to work with horses. Before setting up home with his 'foul-mouthed, pipe-smoking' wife at the Murder Hole, Cushy reputedly lived in a cave at the Back Strand, at Downhill.

It is said that on the occasion in question, Hopkins, who lived in Bolea House, only a mile or two from the Murder Hole, had left The Foxhunters' Arms, situated at number 4 New Row, Coleraine, to return home after a good day's business. Cushy Glenn was waiting for him on the desolate moorland road as he travelled home. This time though, when he took on his neighbour, Cushy met his match. This time it was Cushy Glenn who took the fatal shot. Descendants of James Barr, the innkeeper of The Foxhunters' Arms, are said to still have in their possession, the small single shot pistol that William Hopkins used that night.

Some years ago the Coleraine and Limavady Councils agreed to rename the road 'Windyhill Road,' but the much more gruesomely attractive 'Murder Hole Road' is still commonly used. Locals can still point out, with absolute conviction, the Murder Hole where Cushy's victims were dumped, 200 years ago.

Revolution and the United Irishmen

In the closing decades of the 18th century, there was growing discontent among Catholics and Presbyterians looking for reform of the Penal Laws and Parliament. The American War of Independence and the French Revolution would set powerful examples which, increasingly in the period, seemed to pose a serious threat to the despotic rule of monarchies across Europe. Privilege itself, and the entire premise on which government was organised in the age, came under attack. For the government in Ireland, the situation was to be further complicated by the fact that the regular army was preoccupied with the American War in the 1770's. Since Ireland was left largely undefended, a new Irish Volunteer force was formed. The government provided the new corps with arms and the Limavady Battalion of the Irish Volunteers was formed on 7th November 1777. James Boyle was appointed Colonel of the new force which wore a uniform of scarlet, faced with black. In October the following year the Derry merchant, Andrew Ferguson, ordered sixty muskets and bayonets from a Birmingham gunsmith for the Newtown Limavady Volunteers. Each musket was to be numbered, from one to sixty, in addition to having the letters 'Nn Ly Volunteer' inscribed on it. The rapid growth of the new force in the

province presented its own problems and it very quickly
seemed capable of posing a threat to the government that
had authorised it. In June 1781, when the Rt. Hon. Thomas
Conolly passed through Dungiven, he was saluted by the
Dungiven Corps of Volunteers drawn up to receive him. As
he proceeded on towards Limavady he would be escorted
the last two miles into the town by around two hundred
of his Limavady freehold tenants, all mounted, together
with the Bovevagh and Myroe Corps of Volunteers. The
popularity of the Volunteers and their political aims began
to concern the government to the extent that it decided to
pass an Arms Act, which effectively abolished the force.
A new militia, formed to replace the Volunteers, was to

Wolfe Tone

prove essential in the coming years, as the growing political uncertainty led towards an
attempted revolution.

On the evening of the 11th October 1791, Theobald Wolfe Tone, a Protestant lawyer
from Dublin, arrived in Belfast to advise northern reformers on how best to press for
rapid political reform. He had come to their attention through a widely circulated and
popular article he had written in September 1791, entitled 'Argument on Behalf of
the Catholics of Ireland.' Three days after his arriving in Belfast, the Society of United
Irishmen was founded in a tavern in Crown Entry, off High Street. It sought to unite 'all
the people of Ireland' of every religious persuasion. In January 1792 the organisation
launched its own journal, the Northern Star, and its ideals spread quickly from Belfast
to neighbouring towns in Antrim and Down. The movement spread north too, with a
Society being formed in Ballymoney in 1795. Uncertain of their precise programme
and intentions, the Belfast reformers were nonetheless enthusiastic patriots. It was they
who had organised the festival that O'Hampsey attended in Belfast. The Belfast Harp
Festival was specifically arranged to coincide with the Bastille Day commemorations of
1792 as they sought to stimulate a revival of Irish traditional music. The event marked
the beginning of a long association between northern Protestants and the Gaelic revival.
After attending a performance of the harpers in the Assembly Rooms and perhaps
having listened to O'Hampsey himself, Tone noted the significance of the occasion in
his personal journal with the words, "Strum and be hanged."

Support for the ideals of the French Revolution was increasingly evident. In 1791,
two years after the French Revolution, both Derry and Limavady celebrated Bastille Day.
At the time of the Festival, in July 1792, it was reported that subscribers from Coleraine

and Limavady had sent £600 to the President of the French National Assembly. The money was to help the French 'in a War in which they were threatened by the Emperor of Germany and the King of Prussia.' In September 1796, Henry Haslett, who had worked in Limavady and had family in the area, was arrested in Belfast and imprisoned because of his connection with the United Irishmen movement. Haslett was the son of a prosperous farmer and linen dealer from Drumneechy. He had worked in the grocery and drapery trade in Limavady before becoming a tea and wine merchant in Belfast. For a time he had edited the Northern Star. There was an underlying sympathy for the movement in the wider area and by 1791 it had over 8,000 members in neighbouring Derry alone. By 1797 membership in Ulster had risen to 120,000 and harsh measures were taken to prevent the movement's spread. As French armies swept from victory to victory in Europe, the government saw the need to make concessions in Ireland. In 1792 Catholics won the right to enter the legal profession and the right to vote followed the year after. The government wisely feared the ties that the Society of United Irishmen were forming between the northern radicals and Catholics.

The organisation had begun to exert some influence on the situation, but as the nature of the French Revolution changed and as Britain was drawn into the conflict, the United Irishmen seemed more and more like traitors than idealists. Eventually, the Irish Parliament passed an Insurrection Act which gave the Lord Lieutenant the authority to place any district under martial law, if he deemed it necessary. The populace in any given district would be compelled to produce their arms to the authorities and the penalty for administering the oath of the United Irishmen was death. For actually taking the oath, the punishment was 'transportation' for life. Suspects could be seized and sent to serve in the Navy.

When a regiment of United Irishmen was formed in Limavady, with William Simpson of Ballycrum as its Major, the local 'gentlemen' became alarmed. In January 1797, Conolly McCausland described how he had assisted Sir George Hill, the Derry M.P., and Lord Cavan, in a sweep of the Roe Valley from Limavady to Dungiven with twenty Derry yeomanry, some Derry cavalry, eighty-five Kerry militia and a few Aberdeen Fencibles. The areas of Dungiven, Gelvin, Bovevagh, Legavalan and Drummond were searched. Out ten hours without stopping, they confiscated ninety-five guns, seven bayonets and sundry pistols. Hill was more than delighted and believed he had the supporters of the United Irishmen in the district "flying to the mountains in all directions." He was aware of some seeking refuge in County Antrim and wrote to Dublin in February, detailing how he would officially serve notice on those absent from their homes, requiring them to serve in the Navy when they were eventually apprehended.

When the rebellion broke there does not seem to have been a rising in the town, though this may have been forestalled by the arrest of several people in the area shortly beforehand, perhaps even up to one hundred men. Information coming to Hill led to the arrest of eleven men in the 'neighbourhood of Newtown Limavady' in April 1797. He became aware that most of the supporters of the organisation in the area were wealthy and well respected men in the community, including amongst them, some ministers. The Reverend Robert Steel of Scriggan congregation, Bovevagh, pleaded guilty to treason and had to leave the country. As well as Major William Simpson, a Lieutenant-Colonel, four captains and several others from the locality were lifted and found guilty of membership. John Scott, an apothecary, along with a woollen draper called Moore, were tried in Neilson's hotel in Derry and sentenced to 500 lashes each. At his trial on the 25th June 1798, James Caldwell of Gortgarn refused to break the oath and was sentenced to 1,000 lashes and 'transportation.' He claimed the pikes he had in his possession had been procured for him by his brother from someone in Limavady called Stevenson, or from Stevenson's workmen. Major William Simpson's property was sold along with that of a John Moore, possibly the woollen draper mentioned above. The sentences for all the men involved were commuted from 'death' sentences to 'transportation.' This usually meant they would be shipped off as convicts to one of the colonies. The money from the sale of their property was later repaid to the owners though, as it was claimed the proceedings of the court martial had not been properly conducted. Simpson managed to get permission to leave the country to begin a new life in America and was allowed back to the area around March 1799 to settle his affairs before leaving definitively. Several gentlemen in the area signed a petition at the time asking for him to be allowed to stay on. He had, they claimed, used his position as an officer in the United Irishmen to prevent a rising in Limavady, but their petition met with no success.

Meanwhile, working tirelessly for the organisation, Wolfe Tone found his way to Paris where he convinced the French to support the United Irishmen with a landing in Ireland. A formidable fleet carrying 14,450 soldiers, and with Tone himself aboard, arrived in Bantry Bay in December 1796. A combination of confusion and bad weather prevented a landing and when subsequent sorties were attempted, these too failed. Tone did not relent though and returned with ten warships to land at Lough Swilly in Donegal, on the 3rd November 1798. He had no success this time either. When he stepped ashore dressed as a French officer on the 3rd November, it was as a prisoner. He had been met and recognised by Sir George Hill, who subsequently dispatched him to Dublin where he was condemned to death. Denied the military execution he desired, Tone slit his own throat in prison and died on 19th November 1798.

It seems to have been around this time that Sir George Hill may have intercepted a large body of United Irishmen near the Roe Bridge who were coming from Belfast and heading in the direction of Derry and Innishowen. It had become the practice of supporters of the organisation to gather in huge numbers to dig the potatoes of those who had been arrested, and it seems this group were assembled under this pretext when Hill challenged them.

5

Progress and Poverty –
The Roe Valley in the 1800's

The Martello Tower

WITH AN INVASION OF Ireland by the French a real possibility, coastal defences were strengthened. The Martello Tower at Magilligan, built in 1812, was part of a series of defensive towers. The design for the towers was based on the Mortello Tower in Sicily, which had resisted days of bombardment by the British navy in 1794. Around forty of the seventy-four towers which were built in Ireland now survive and indeed a similar one exists in Greencastle on the other side of the Lough.

The threat was real. Wolfe Tone's huge French force had only narrowly avoided landing in Bantry Bay in 1796 and in August 1798, during the United Irishmen's Rebellion, 1,000 French soldiers did actually land in Killala, Co. Mayo. Tone's arrest in Donegal, in November 1798, only served to underline the urgent need for better defences. The British were not to know it at the time, but by 1803 Napoleon had abandoned thoughts of an invasion of either England or Ireland.

Strategically sited in coastal locations, these towers were intended to be capable of firing on any invading fleet and of withstanding a lengthy siege. The Magilligan Tower was originally positioned on the beach, but land movement has since altered this. Little about the tower has changed over time despite it having been occupied by the British Army well into the 20th century.

The Martello Tower, Magilligan

The impressive walls, built of dressed sandstone brought from Ballyharrigan Quarries in Bovevagh, are thirteen feet thick and protect a domed circular chamber thirty feet in diameter. Nowadays, entrance to the tower is via an iron staircase which replaces the original wooden ladder that would have been used. Inside, it has three floors. The top floor was intended to support a twenty-pounder gun able to swivel and fire in any direction. A small furnace set into the wall was used to heat the shot and increase the chances of it setting light to the wooden ships they were intended to hit. The living quarters for one officer and twelve men were on the middle floor, with a winding staircase leading to a cellar below, where there was storage space for food and gunpowder. In the event of coming under siege, the tower was also equipped with a well in the cellar. The Tower is now in the care of the National Trust and is conveniently placed for a quick visit, as passengers wait for the ferry to Donegal which docks only a few metres from it.

Ballykelly

Little attention seems to have been given to Ballykelly in the 1700's. The original Walworth House built in 1705 had been so neglected that Barr Beresford, in one of his letters of complaint, sent a piece of its rotten roof to the London Committee of the Fishmongers, in an attempt to highlight its poor state of repair. By the end of the century, the Earl Bishop was bringing some degree of change and improvement when he erected the parish church in 1795, but it would not be until much later, as late as the 1820's, that Ballykelly would undergo a transformation.

In 1824, Church Hill was built to serve as a model farm for its tenants on the Fishmongers' estate. Now extended and enlarged, it operates as the North West Independent Hospital.

On the other side of the road sits Ballykelly Presbyterian Church which was built in 1827. Thackeray, the famous writer and traveller was very impressed by the architecture of the Church when he saw it for the first time in 1842. Close by, the Fishmongers built their agent's house. This is now part of the Drummond House Hotel. At the other edge of the village they built Bridge House as a Dispensary, knocking down the 'wretched mud cabins' that previously occupied the site. The Fishmongers' Coat of Arms, originally located above the door of the Dispensary, is now to be found in the porch of the Drummond House Hotel. It was made in 1829 by J.G. Bubb of London.

The improvements continued with a grain market being planned with sheds and a courtyard, though it is not certain that this was actually built and the Reverend G.V. Sampson, the Fishmongers' agent, planned a canal to transport agricultural produce from the village to the Lough. The work for this was done between 1821 and 1823

The former Model Farm, now the North West Independent Hospital.

Top: Ballykelly Presbyterian Church

Bottom: The four terraced houses on Ballykelly Main Street

by embanking the Ballykelly River from the bridge to the high water mark, but the canal silted up and was never a success. Richard Suitor, the Fishmongers' surveyor, and James Turnbull of Limavady, planned the new buildings, but it was Turnbull who built the Presbyterian Church, Drummond House, Bridge House, and the Lancastrian Schools that were also constructed at the time. Of note as well on the village Main Street is the attractive set of four terraced houses. Built by the Fishmongers in 1825, they still manage to catch the eye to this day.

John Steinbeck

The much admired Ballykelly Presbyterian Church was built at a cost of £4,000, using Dungiven sandstone. It would be almost identical to the design Richard Suitor used on Banagher Church, which was also built on the Fishmongers' lands. In the October of 1830, three years after Ballykelly Presbyterian Church was built, a Samuel Hamilton was baptized there.

This young man would eventually emigrate to New York at the age of seventeen and marry a young Irish girl called Elizabeth Fagen in 1849. Together they would set off for California, via the Isthmus of Panama. By so doing, they were avoiding what would have been an even more treacherous trek across America to the west coast. The couple eventually settled on a farm of 1,760 acres near King City in the Salinas Valley. Sam Hamilton wasn't perhaps to fully comprehend it, but his links with Ballykelly would later prove very important to his famous grandson, John Steinbeck. Hamilton was the maternal grandfather of the Nobel Prize winning author, and it was this connection that brought Steinbeck back to Ballykelly with his wife Elaine in August 1952. Searching for Ballykelly, Steinbeck imagined he was looking for a town and drove through it to Limavady, before realising the reason for his error. He would later write:

"It's what they call in Texas, a wide place in the road."

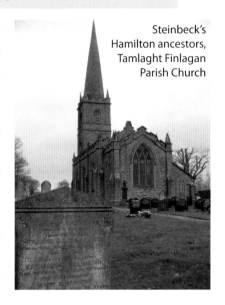
Steinbeck's Hamilton ancestors, Tamlaght Finlagan Parish Church

In an article in Colliers' Magazine in January 1953, Steinbeck described his visit to Ballykelly and Ballykelly Presbyterian Church. He is shown photographed beside the graves of his Hamilton ancestors in the grounds of Tamlaght Finlagan Parish Church, which is situated just opposite the Presbyterian Church.

The Hamilton farm in the Salinas Valley was to appear many times in his fiction. The 'ranch' provides the setting for 'The Red Pony' and Samuel Hamilton assumes a central role in Steinbeck's classic, 'East of Eden', which was published in September 1952, the month after Steinbeck was in Ballykelly. Steinbeck was proud of his Irish roots:

"I am half Irish, the rest of my blood being watered down with German and Massachusetts English. But Irish blood doesn't water down very well; the strain must be very strong."

The highly reputed author only narrowly missed his last surviving aunt in Ireland, Mary Elizabeth (Minnie) Hamilton, who died in February 1950 aged eighty-four, at Mulkeeragh. She was the daughter of William John Hamilton, Samuel Hamilton's brother.

The 'Roe Valley' Hamilton farm was located near Mulkeeragh Wood, just off the Tully Road. Steinbeck's connections with Ballykelly and the locality seem to have been very important to him. As he put it himself, it was there that he was able to experience:

Steinbeck's novel, The Red Pony

"the seat of my culture and the origin of my being and the soil of my background, the one full-blown evidence of a thousand years of family."

The Ordnance Survey of Ireland

In the autumn of 1824, a team of Royal Engineer officers, sappers and miners, under the command of Major General Thomas F. Colby, arrived in Ireland to undertake the first Ordnance Survey mapping of Ireland. Civil servants and scholars were assigned to help with the sketching, drawing, and engraving of maps, and in writing accompanying notes and descriptive accounts. Interestingly, the man employed by Colby as the Head of the Topographical Department (Antiquities Division) from 1833 until 1843, was George Petrie. It would be to this very same

Major General T.F. Colby

George Petrie that Jane Ross would forward the 'Londonderry Air' or 'Danny Boy' just a few years later.

Colby chose to begin this vast undertaking by setting an eight mile long baseline that would run from Ballykelly to Magilligan. This area was found suitable because of the large expanse of level ground available and because it could be most easily tied in with a similar project in Scotland. The baseline towers he used are still in situ in Magilligan and Ballykelly, with the south base Ballykelly tower being particularly easy to visit.

Ballykelly Ordnance Survey Base Tower

This tower marks the end of the baseline and is situated at the edge of the playing fields, behind the King's Lane estate. A plaque in the grounds of the Drummond Hotel also records the important undertaking. The work would involve highly precise measurements and to protect the baselines the Survey engineers purchased the land on which they sat. In the Magilligan area they bought land from Mr Gage at a cost of two guineas and erected two stone base towers, one at Minearny and one at Ballymulholland. Though located on private land, these are still in existence. A fourth tower was built at Mount Sandy on the shoreline of the Magilligan/Benone Strand, but it has since been claimed by the sea. The tower bases each house a platina wire set in lead and concrete. The platina wire has a mark made in it, directly above which is an edged cross on a metal plate set on a flagstone. To establish height levels the surveyors set up various crow's foot 'benchmarks,' one of

Survey marker at the Point Bar

which can be seen on the retained façade of Limavady Town Hall. Another is carved into a large boulder on the highest point on Benbradagh mountain. Yet another bench mark for the survey can be seen outside The Point Bar at Magilligan. This takes the form of a small pointed pillar which has the familiar crow's foot symbol on it as well as the numbers 3.11, indicating the height in feet, above sea level.

The aim of the survey was to provide maps for the valuation of Ireland to support the local taxation system. Completed on a scale of six inches to the mile, the maps were large enough to show townlands and boundaries.

Ireland would be the first country to be completely mapped on such a large scale. At least two of the Royal Engineers who came over with the survey ended up marrying locally. The two daughters of Robert Conn, Margaret and Isabella, who lived in the Lodge at the time, married William Lancey and Robert Fenwick. Some time later the Lancey family would go on to live in the Lodge.

The Survey was carried out between the years 1824 and 1846 under Colby's direction. He knew that the most important part of the triangulation for the Survey was the determination of scale using a precise base. In 1824 he selected a site for this base on the flat eastern shore of Lough Foyle. It was to be the longest of its kind and would be measured to a standard of accuracy never before achieved anywhere in the world. Colby invented an original apparatus to carry out the measurement. He devised

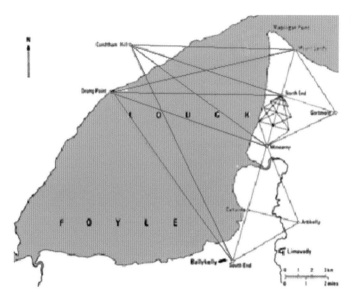

Plan of the Survey

a compensation bar of iron and brass about ten feet long between pivots which would always remain the same length, unaffected by temperature change. Measurement of the base, initially under Colby's supervision, began on 6th September 1827, but later proceeded under the direction of Lieutenant Thomas Drummond, one of the Survey's leading mathematicians. The work was completed on 20th November 1828, having taken the most part of two summers to complete. The length of the base, levelled and reduced to the adjoining sea level, was 41,640 feet or nearly eight miles.

A subsequent base line was measured out in 1849 at Salisbury Plain in England using the same apparatus and methods that Colby had perfected in Ireland. This was then connected to the Lough Foyle base through the principal triangulation network. In 1960 the Ordnance Survey of Northern Ireland re-measured the Ballykelly and Magilligan base using electronic equipment and, to the great credit of the 19th century surveyors, found a difference of only one inch in the calculations.

Born in Edinburgh in 1797, Thomas Drummond was to become an important figure in his own right. After seeing a demonstration of the effect of 'limelight' given by Michael Faraday, Drummond built a working version of a 'limelight' in 1826 to help him with the Survey work. In an experiment to test his 'Drummond Light,' he set one up on Slieve Snaught in Donegal and found, as he had predicted, that it was visible some sixty-six miles away, on Divis Mountain above Belfast. The exceptionally bright luminescent light was the result of burning a block of lime in a hot hydrogen and oxygen flame. He later adapted it for use in lighthouses and it came to be widely used as a spotlight in theatres across the world in the 1860's and 70's, despite there being a very real danger of it causing an explosion. It is from its use in this way in theatres that we get the phrase being 'in the limelight.' When a Boundary Commission was set up to ensure fairly apportioned parliamentary constituencies as a result of the 1832 Reform Act, Drummond was put in charge of it and he later served as Under Secretary of State in Ireland. In 1838 he famously pointed out to absentee landlords that "property has its duties as well as its rights." Heading up a Commission on railways in 1835, Drummond pioneered railway development in Ireland too, but his network plans were never implemented.

Eglinton

In common with Ballykelly and other settlements in the area, Eglinton benefited from a period of renewed interest and investment on the part of the London Companies in the 1800's. Much of the charm of the neat little tree-lined village of to-day comes from buildings erected in this period.

In the centre of the village, the Court and Market House, built between 1823 and 1827, particularly captures the 'English' appearance of the place. Designed by Michael Angelo Nicholson, it originally had open arcades on the ground floor for the market. Low walls next to it bear the Coat of Arms, on the left side, of the Babington family, and on the right side, of the Grocers' Company. The Manor House and the Glen House also date from this period and provide evidence of the growing vitality of the village at the time. A row of cottages now known as Cottage Row, was built in this period for widows,

Babington Coat of Arms

The Grocers' Company Coat of Arms

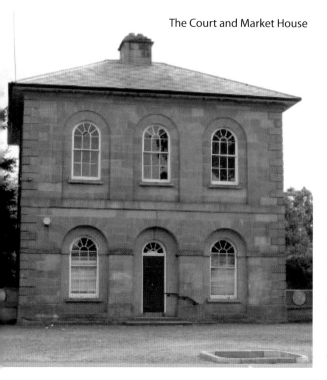

The Court and Market House

along with tradesmen's houses which were constructed on the main street. Also on the main street, located beside the former National School, is the former Erasmus Smith schoolhouse which was built in 1812 and is now a private home. An Agricultural School at Templemoyle, set up with the intention of teaching new agricultural techniques, was opened in 1826. Some time later, in 1858, when the Lord Lieutenant of Ireland, the Earl of Eglinton and Winton visited the School, the name of the village was officially changed to 'Eglinton,' in his honour. The inhabitants had long been petitioning for a name change for the village from its original name of Muff. Several settlements with the same name had grown up in the area and the village's mail had frequently gone by mistake to another Muff, in nearby Donegal. The adopted name has remained unaltered since. The pleasant appearance of Eglinton was further enhanced in the 20th century by the addition of two oaks trees in the village street brought from Windsor Great Park as saplings and planted there to commemorate the coronation of Edward VII in June 1902 and that of George V, in June 1911.

Dungiven

In 1794, Colonel Edward Carey sold the lease of Dungiven to Robert Ogilby, a Dublin linen merchant, for £10,000. When Ogilby obtained a new lease from the Skinners' Company for a lump sum payment of £25,000 and a yearly rent of £1,500, he then set about improving Dungiven. In 1819 he donated the land on which the Roman Catholic Church was built. A quarter of the overall cost of this building would be raised from the Protestants living in the area, and after donating the land, Ogilby subsequently made a further cash donation of £35 towards the Church. Following this, he built a schoolhouse in 1823 and paid for the rebuilding of the town's hotel in the 1830's. Ogilby was entitled to charge tolls on the goods bought and sold in the local market, but after building a market house and yard costing £1,000, he removed these tolls before opening the market house on 31st December 1829. By 1834, Dungiven was a town with a population of over 1,000 inhabitants and around 180 houses. He seems to have given some attention as well to the houses in the town, which were kept 'constantly white-washed and in good repair.' Reports of the time claim the older inhabitants were pleased with the improvements to the place, which not that long before, had only 'a few wretched cabins.' While he was living in Pellipar House, Robert Ogilby spent vast sums of money on rebuilding the town castle. Despite this, when he died in 1839, it was still neither completed nor occupied.

His nephew, Robert Leslie Ogilby, succeeded him and continued the improvements. While the houses of the town actually belonged to the estate of the new landlord, Robert Leslie allowed his tenants to buy and sell their own homes. This encouraged many of the new owners to bring about their own improvements and by 1860 most of the houses had replaced thatch roofs with slate roofs.

With Robert Ogilby having made his fortune exporting linen, it is not surprising that Dungiven's economy became dependent on this industry. Three quarters of all the men of Scottish and English Planter descent were estimated to be employed in weaving and manufacturing linen in 1814 and during the winter months all families would have sought to earn extra cash from spinning. The decline in the linen trade however, and the subsequent famine, would inevitably bring about dramatic changes in the Dungiven economy. New ways of earning a living evolved, and as the century progressed, we find that cattle dealing, for example, began to play an increasingly important role in the area.

Drenagh House and Charles Lanyon

No doubt the increased activity of the London Companies in the county generally during the period, attracted the attention of the residents of the 'Great Houses' in our area. Perhaps this had an influence on the decision to rebuild Drenagh House, situated on Drenagh Estate on the edge of Limavady town. Originally called Fruithill, the first house on the land was built in the 1730's. The estate, along with that of Roe Park, or Daisy Hill as it was then known, came to the McCausland family as a gift to Robert McCausland from William Conolly. Robert had worked as Conolly's agent and was generously given the property as an acknowledgement of the "faithful services he has done me." His son, Conolly McCausland, inherited Fruithill and then his son in turn, also known as Conolly, lived in the house which was located in the centre of a well-

Drenagh House

wooded parkland. Even after some extension work the original house was felt to be too small by the 1820's and drawings for a new building were commissioned from a Mr John Hargrave. These were never executed, though they still survive and show a neo-Greek design for the new house, which bears a resemblance to Seaforde House in Co. Down. The idea for a new building was left until Charles Lanyon arrived in County Antrim as county surveyor in 1835/6. Lanyon was to carve out a considerable career for himself in his chosen profession and Drenagh appears to have been his very first commission for a country house of major proportions.

From the restrained neo-classicism of Drenagh, he would progress through Laurel Hill in Coleraine, in 1843, to evolve a sumptuous and assured Italianate style for Dundarave House, in 1847. The interior plan of the house is indeed similar to that of Dundarave's and also to that of Ballywalter Park. Drenagh is now open to the public, providing elegant surroundings for conferences, and private functions with luxurious accommodation. There is also the opportunity to view a painting of the original owner of the estate, Robert McCausland, with the 1730's house visible in the background.

Lanyon would become Ulster's most important architect of the Victorian era. By the time of his death in 1889 he had designed a host of buildings across the province and, most notably, in Belfast. Lanyon designed the main building of Queen's University, Belfast Castle, The Palm House at Botanic Gardens, Crumlin Road Gaol, the Linenhall Library and the Customs House. The list is long, impressive and diverse and includes bridges and viaducts and even the 1,500 Scots Pines planted in 1839 that form the picturesque Frosses Trees. Lanyon was knighted in 1868, having served as Mayor of Belfast and as a Conservative M.P. for the city from 1865 to 1868.

Bellarena or Ballymargy House

Lanyon was also employed at Bellarena, originally known as Ballymargy House, Magilligan, for the redecoration of the reception rooms and a staircase and to add a new porch. It seems most likely that the house has been on the same site since the 1600's and that a section of the present building dates from that period. While the house was altered and added to by successive owners, both in 1797 and again in 1822, the property includes one of the most complete sets of farm buildings appropriate to the running of a large 19th century estate.

The Famine and Limavady Workhouse

One of Limavady's finest landmarks is its former Workhouse, situated only a short walk from the town centre. Beautifully restored and managed by Limavady Community Development Initiative, the Workhouse building was originally constructed in 1841 for the purpose of housing the area's poor and needy. The Limavady Workhouse formed part of a network of such buildings that covered the entire length and breadth of Ireland. Limavady's example remains virtually intact since this period making it a unique treasure, not just within the Borough, but also within the wider context of Ireland's history and built heritage.

Before 1838, there was no general provision for those who could not cater for themselves. Certain towns provided specific help such as for 'vagrants' in Houses of Industry, or for 'children' in foundling hospitals, or for 'the old' in homes like the Belfast Charitable Institution. From 1832 Limavady had a charitable Poor Shop set up to help 'the lower orders.' It was set up on the 18th October 1832 by 'a few individuals anxious for the temporal welfare of the poor inhabitants' in the Limavady area. Buchanans, who had their premises in Linenhall Street from 1832-62, printed up the regulations concerning its operation. Three ladies, resident in the town or in the parish of Drumachose, would preside over the business of the Shop from 11 a.m. to 3 p.m. on Tuesdays. To begin with, it was thought that forty or fifty pounds worth of clothes would get the charity underway and that it should start off by confining itself to the Parish of Drumachose only. The clothes would be sold off at cost price and could be bought by instalments of a penny a week – though a 'respectable person' would have to vouch for the buyer in the first instance.

The Poor Shop regulations make reference to following the model of other such organisations which already operated successfully throughout the country. As was the case for Limavady's Poor Shop, these shops were usually supported by subscription and charity. There were some notable exceptions to this. Cork Foundling Home for example, was supported by a tax on coal landed in the port and several Dublin institutions were supported by Parliamentary grant.

The Poor Law Act of 1838 introduced a universal Poor Law system for the whole of Ireland. It was a system that had already been operating in England, but with one important difference. In England, relief was often given as 'out' relief, which did not require the recipients to enter the Workhouse. Relief inside the workhouse was optional in England. The Irish system however made 'out-relief' illegal, and would only permit 'in-relief.'

NEWTOWNLIMAVADY
POOR SHOP.

A few individuals, anxious for the temporal welfare of the poor Inhabitants of this Town and Parish, have determined, with the blessing of the Almighty, to form in it a Poor Shop for the benefit of the lower orders, which they purpose conducting according to the following Regulations, adopted and acted upon with great advantage to the poorer classes, by other institutions of a similar nature in different parts of this country :—

1.—A sufficient quantity to commence with of such articles of Clothing or Bedding, &c. &c. as may be considered most serviceable for the use of the Poor, is to be laid in immediately; and for this purpose it is intended to appeal to the charitable feelings of all who are interested about the well-being of the lower orders, to assist in this design with their voluntary contributions, which they are requested to continue from year to year afterwards, according as they see the object in view beneficial or otherwise in its results.

2.—The articles for sale are to be purchased of the most serviceable quality, and at the same time at the most reasonable rate, from Shopkeepers in this Town or elsewhere, as may seem most advantageous to the Managers of this Institution, and they will be sold out to the Poor at first cost price, under the following conditions.

3.—When any person wishes to purchase an article at the Poor Shop, they must bring a respectable person along with them as their security, who will pass his or her word for them that they will pay for the goods purchased, or else become subject themselves to the payment of the amount that is due, in case of the non-payment of the purchaser within such period of time as the Managers shall consider sufficiently lengthened to discharge the debt incurred.

4.—The article purchased is to be paid for by weekly instalments of a Penny in the Shilling; and when the debt is discharged, an acknowledgement for the receipt of the amount is to be given by one of the Managers on the purchaser's ticket.

5.—When an article is given out, a ticket is given to the purchaser with the amount mentioned upon it.— This ticket is brought by the purchaser every day of payment, when the amount paid is entered upon the ticket until the debt is cleared, and then the aforementioned acknowledgement is made upon the ticket, and it is returned to the owner.

6.—A person not making a payment for three weeks in succession is fined One Penny, which is to be added to the amount of their debt.

7.—Three Ladies chosen from among the Managers, and residents in the Town of Newtown, or in the Parish of Drumachose, convenient to the Town, are to preside at the Poor Shop, to give out Clothes, &c. once a week, from 11 o'clock till 3; and it is considered that at present Tuesday will be the best day for the purpose.

8.—As the aforementioned individuals have no other motive in view but the welfare of the lower orders in this Town and Parish, it is expected that such ideas of their intentions will be pressed upon the poorer classes by persons of influence over them, and that such persons will use every effort in their power to promote the welfare and interest of this Institution.

9.—It is purposed to confine the advantages of this Poor Shop to the Parish of Drumachose for a year or two at least, until the Managers see how it succeeds.

The business of the Shop will be conducted as has been mentioned by three Ladies, chosen out of a Committee of Managers. A confidential Secretary and Treasurer will keep the accounts, and be answerable for the proper disposal of the money entrusted to their care by the Subscribers to the Poor Shop's Fund.

Forty or Fifty Pounds worth of Goods will be required to commence with, which sum it is hoped will be raised in this Parish by voluntary contributions.

N. B.—You are requested to attend to the above communication, and are respectfully informed that an early application will be made to you for your contribution in aid of this benevolent Institution.

Newtownlimavady, October 18, 1832,

GEORGE BUCHANAN, PRINTER, NEWTOWNLIMAVADY.

Newtownlimavady Poor Shop regulations

Experienced English Poor Law Commissioners travelled to Ireland to set up the new system. They divided the country into one hundred and thirty Unions, broadly based on the various market towns. Each Union was controlled by a Board of Guardians, which met weekly. As well as having 'elected' guardians, the Boards had resident magistrates serving on them as 'ex-officio' guardians. The able-bodied who entered the workhouse were expected to pay for this relief with their labour. In practice, it proved difficult to provide sufficient suitable tasks for them all on a regular basis. Many workhouses specialised in different activities such as stone breaking to make roads. It has been suggested that shoe making may have been the speciality in the Limavady Workhouse, but for the moment this is based only rather loosely on oral evidence. A visitor to Newtownlimavady's 'model' workhouse in 1870 wrote in The Irish Builder that rearing pigs was its principal source of revenue. The writer was struck by the good economy exercised by the Guardians in keeping a horse and three cows and maintaining their own five acre farm.

The Boards of Guardians were given powers to raise funds through the collection of 'poor rates.' This was due from every house, including rented houses, and was based on a valuation known as the Poor Law Valuation, which is a term that stayed with us until quite recently. Following his visit in 1870, the writer of the article in The Irish Builder calculated that the rates burden on the ratepayers of Limavady was around 30 % lower than that imposed in other Unions in Ulster, because of good management. The Poor Law Commissioners had originally hoped to use the staff of the Board of Public Works to design and build the workhouses, but this proved to be legally impossible. George Wilkinson of Oxford eventually won the contract and was appointed in 1839. He had built a number of workhouses for English Unions and was engaged initially for one year as Commissioners' architect. He was to be retained until 1855 however and built a further thirty-three workhouses, to take the number in Ireland to one hundred and sixty-three in total. The workhouse buildings were almost all built to a standard plan and came in three different sizes. The small workhouse was to cater for between two and three hundred inmates, the middle size for between four and six hundred, and the large for one thousand or more inmates. All were to be capable of expansion, should the need arise, to hold a further one to two hundred inmates. The cost of Irish workhouses was only two thirds that of similar workhouses in England and Wales. The reduction in cost was achieved by making the floors of mortar or earth instead of timber or flagstones, and by making sleeping platforms. These were nothing more than raised wooden floors on both sides of the wards. Here, the inmates would sleep on straw mattresses instead

Limavady Workhouse

of beds. This saved space as well. The rough stone walls were whitewashed and left unplastered, with the dormitory having no ceiling, just bare rafters.

Wilkinson managed to cut costs, as requested, but did so bearing in mind the visual impact the buildings were likely to have on the small 'market town' architecture of Ireland. He endeavoured to minimise this impact by using local stone, in the hope that it would more easily blend in with its background. He was aware that in many cases the buildings would have to occupy a "necessarily conspicuous situation." To counter this, he chose a style which he considered "the least obtrusive," using "gabled roofs and elevated chimney shafts" to give the buildings "a picturesque and pleasing appearance." This was entirely typical of the early Victorian period, when architects often favoured styles based on their association with the past. The building style of the workhouse has clear references to the alms-houses of Tudor and Jacobean England.

The Poor Law Union of Newtownlimavady was set up in September 1839 and covered an area of 150,000 acres. The Board of Guardians comprised eight ex-officio guardians: Marcus McCausland, Robert Ogilby, David Cather, John B. Beresford, Connolly Gage, Arthur Sampson, John Given, and James Stevenson, and twenty-three elected guardians: John Hunter, Henry Tyler, Marcus Gage, John Canning, Edward Boyle, Alexander Morrison, James Douglas, William Osborne, Thomas McCully, Thomas Ross, Robert

Kydd, John Scott, Stewart Bruce, John Stevenson, Michael Ross, James Quig, Robert Barbour, Samuel Craig, James Stirling, James Dunn, James Stuart, James Reynolds and Lachlan J McCurdy.

They had their first recorded meeting on 28th October 1839, electing Marcus McCausland as their chairman, and appointing the Northern Bank as the treasurers of the Union. A sub-committee comprising the chairman, Connolly Gage, John B. Beresford, Robert Ogilby and Arthur Sampson, found a site of 7.26 acres on the outskirts of the town, which was purchased in December 1839 for £708 5s from Michael King of Dungiven. Three months later a strip of land sixteen feet wide was bought from Frederick McCausland of Bessbrook, for £55, to make a roadway out to the Dungiven Road. In June 1840 the contract was given to a Mr McCarter of Derry for a medium size workhouse, that is, one that would hold four hundred inmates, but that could be extended to hold six hundred, if required.

It was to be completed by August 1841, but the first inmate was not received until 15th March 1842. It had cost £5,982, with a further £1,309 5 shillings going on fittings and contingencies. Frederick Smith from Derry supplied the furnishings and Hugh McCawley of Limavady made the wooden furniture. The bedding along with the furniture cost £220 12s 10d. The bedding consisted of a blanket, a coverlet, a one third sheet, a bedtick, and two bolster ticks per bed. By December of 1843 it was operating with 100 inmates. This was in a town with a population of 3,101 in 1841 that had once again experienced a bout of cholera. A rate of twenty pence was struck and this was sufficient to meet costs. The food bill was set at £12 per week initially and remained at this, even when numbers rose to two hundred inmates.

The Guardians employed eleven people to run the workhouse, appointing Dr Lane as Medical Officer on £40 per annum and Mr James Murphy as the Master, on a similar salary. Mrs Murphy was employed as Matron on £25 per year and three chaplains, a clerk, a nurse, a porter, a schoolmaster and schoolmistress made up the remaining staff. With the onset of the Great Famine the entire national workhouse system was to find itself under almost immediate strain.

The Great Famine lasted from 1845 to 1849. At its most simplistic level it can be said to have been brought about by the appearance on the potato crop of a new fungal disease, 'phytophthora infestans,' or 'blight,' as it is commonly called. The reasons behind its staggering effects on Ireland are decidedly complex however. From 1800 to 1841 the population of Ireland went from five million to over eight million people, making it one of the most densely populated countries in Europe. Traditionally in Ireland, farmers had subdivided their land between their sons. This rise in population meant subdivision inevitably led to families living on an acreage of land too small to be viable. This in turn encouraged people to grow potatoes, as this was a crop that was just about sustainable in these conditions. On average, a person ate seven pounds of potatoes a day and even quite a small plot could grow enough to provide for most of the year. There was always a difficult period of at least two months when the old crop had ended and the new one was not ready. During these 'hungry' or 'meal' months they survived on a meal-based porridge. Famines were common in Ireland. There had been a particularly bad one in 1740/41 and there were fourteen partial or complete famines between 1816 and 1842. The famine of 1740 is thought to have been as catastrophic as any famine suffered in the country, but gets little attention because there is scant detail relating to it. What gave the Great Famine its special character was that the crop failed over the whole country, and that the failure was repeated in successive years.

With the potato shortages of 1845 other prices rose. The cost of keeping a pauper in the workhouse rose too. In the space of a year from April 1845 to April 1846 the cost rose

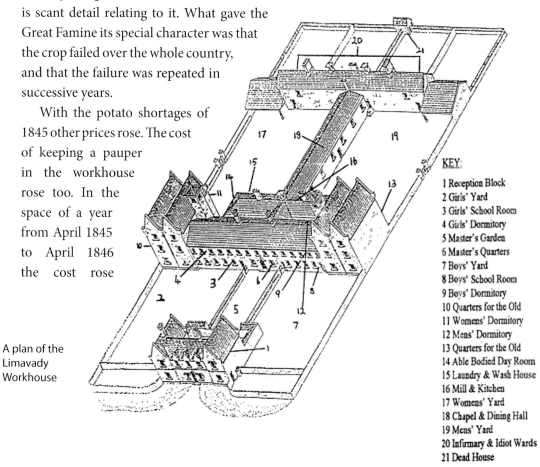

A plan of the Limavady Workhouse

KEY:

1 Reception Block
2 Girls' Yard
3 Girls' School Room
4 Girls' Dormitory
5 Master's Garden
6 Master's Quarters
7 Boys' Yard
8 Boys' School Room
9 Boys' Dormitory
10 Quarters for the Old
11 Womens' Dormitory
12 Mens' Dormitory
13 Quarters for the Old
14 Able Bodied Day Room
15 Laundry & Wash House
16 Mill & Kitchen
17 Womens' Yard
18 Chapel & Dining Hall
19 Mens' Yard
20 Infirmary & Idiot Wards
21 Dead House

from 1s 3½d to 1s 11d. Writing in 1846, the Lord Lieutenant of Londonderry was able to point out that the problem was not an absolute shortage of food in the area. There had been a good oat crop, but food was too expensive for the average labourer to buy, given his rate of pay. In the immediate locality, the construction of the railway from Derry to Coleraine and the consequent reclamation of slob land from Lough Foyle gave employment. The construction of the Dogleap Bridge in the 1840's also used relief labour.

Labourers though, earned between 9d and 10d a day, which was the price of a stone of oats from David Lynch of Bolea in January 1845. By January 1847 it would cost a labourer 2s 1¼d to buy a stone of oats from him, making it more than twice the price it had been two years earlier.

The attitudes of the time placed great value on personal self-reliance and Government interference in society was not normal, nor considered appropriate. This 'laissez-faire' attitude was popular as a policy in the age and it was applied to matters of trade and economics. Some measures were taken though, to relieve the hardship. Sir Robert Peel, the British Prime Minister, secretly bought £100,000 of Indian meal or maize in America and had it shipped to Ireland. 'Peel's Brimstone' was not popular at first with the Irish, but with starvation as the only alternative, it came to be accepted. By January 1847, there were 110,000 in the workhouses meant for 100,000 people. The overcrowding just added to the problems making it easier for diseases to be transmitted and 'famine fever' became widespread. More people died of these diseases than of hunger. Hannah Moore, aged thirty-five from Drum, is recorded as having died of 'Fever' on 20th March 1847 in the Limavady Workhouse and in June it would take Henry McCloskey from Owenreagh, aged forty, Ann McCurdy from Limavady, also aged forty, and eighteen year old Barbara McKeever from Gelvin. Later that same year it was the cause of death of sixty year old Henry Higgins from Myroe, eleven year old Thomas Stewart and seventy year old Grace Lynch, both of Limavady.

In 1846, for a cost of £477, the Limavady Workhouse Guardians asked Robert Boyd to build a Fever Hospital as they sought to deal with the crisis. Public Works Schemes were introduced to provide a basic income for the needy, so that they could then buy food, instead of having to rely on charity. The pay was poor and uncertain though, and the hours were long. Even so, men hung around these work schemes waiting for someone to collapse in the hope of being employed. In October 1846, there were 114,000 employed on works like these. When this rose to 700,000 in February 1847 the Treasury, in the person of Charles Edward Trevelyan, baulked at the growing cost and these schemes were all but ended. Deaths were rising steadily in the country, as were admissions to the workhouses. By the second week of March of 1847, admissions had reached eighty-three per week in the Limavady Workhouse, having started the year at around thirty-seven per week. They were eventually to reach a high point of ninety-seven admissions per week and the Guardians decided to offer outdoor relief to aged and infirm inmates in the form of cooked food such as soup, porridge, or home baked bread. Their intention in doing this was to try to free up more accommodation in the workhouse. The possibility of extending the provision as planned for by Wilkinson had to be made reality and the building was eventually enlarged. The buildings containing the 'idiot' wards were raised and by January 1848 there were 950 paupers in residence. Although there were around seven to eight deaths per week, this was few compared to other parts of the country. With no vaccine in existence, 'Measles' alone killed thirteen children between December 1847 and January 1848 and the Master's Record throughout the period shows a large percentage of those who died in the Workhouse did so of 'Old Age.'

From 1841 to 1931 the Limavady Workhouse paupers were buried in the Scroggy Road burial ground. Originally placed in unmarked graves, the pauper burial site is now marked by a plaque. The long thin plot was placed as far from the main Workhouse building as possible, for fear of spreading the cholera and other highly infectious

The paupers' burial site

diseases to the inmates. A wreath is now placed on the site annually in a memorial service organised by the Limavady Community Development Initiative. The Workhouse played a vital role in the community's attempt to cope with the Famine and it would not be placed under such stress again. It closed its doors to the poor in 1930 when the last twenty healthy inmates were transferred to Coleraine. The old infirmary retained some patients until 1932 and from 1937, after some conversion work, the building operated as the Roe Valley District Hospital. Closing as a Hospital in 1997, it was fully restored by L.C.D.I. and now serves as a modern multi-purpose community facility.

During the height of the Famine, private funds and private charity contributed considerably to the relief of the hardship and suffering. Irishmen in the Indian army, for example, sent a donation of £50,000 and a private committee in Dublin raised £63,000. The Society of Friends or Quakers gave food, clothing and seeds where they were most needed and proved useful also in accurately reporting back the effects of the mounting disaster to England.

Having stopped the work schemes, Trevelyan decided to replace these with a new and less expensive scheme – less expensive, that is, to the government. This time the burden would rest on the local ratepayers who would be expected to provide soup kitchens to feed the starving. The landlords were often less than enthusiastic about this idea as it was they who were meant to pay for it. In consequence, the food was often poor quality and was always ready cooked so that people could not sell the raw ingredients. Anyone with more than a quarter of an acre of land did not qualify for food. The soup was a type of porridge called stirabout and each person was to get one pound per day. In general these worked well, but hardship reached deep into the community. Evidence from Dungiven shows eighteen families being evicted, for falling behind with their rent, between 1848 and 1849. Owing rent arrears of £10 2s 9d, Thomas Gwynne gave up his house in December 1848 and the house he had rented was 'thrown down.' Margaret Morton was evicted in May 1848 owing £10 10 shillings. Having built up arrears of £7 5s 6d in 1845, John Roe McCloskey was evicted and his house was 'thrown down' in November 1845. While limited charity was available from the landlord, some tenants from Dungiven would have had no choice but seek refuge in the Limavady Workhouse when they were evicted.

Following a meeting of the town and parish in Limavady in December 1846, a soup or broth kitchen supported by voluntary contributions was set up, which became operational by January of 1847. The 'Brochan House,' situated beside the Dogleap Bridge at the entrance to the Country Park, was one of the distribution points for this type of stirabout in the area. 'Brochan' is the Irish word for porridge.

By December 1848, the cost of keeping a pauper had begun to drop. The fact that it now cost 1 shilling 2½d, or a full one penny less per week than it had in April 1845, was a clear indication that the worst of the Famine had passed. The north had fared better than the south or west, but not as well as Leinster. The effect varied greatly even within Ulster. Historians try to obtain a truer picture of this effect by calculating 'excess deaths', that is, the number over and above those who would have died from the usual causes. While County Fermanagh had an average annual rate per thousand of 29.2, Donegal had 10.7 and Londonderry only 5.7 by comparison. It is likely that the well-established pattern of seasonal migration and emigration allowed a great many of the destitute to escape, just before the Famine or during its early stages. Many saw emigration as the only hope of staying alive. In an eleven year period, during and after the Famine, Ireland sent abroad over two million people, more than had emigrated over the preceding two and a half centuries. Ulster provided 40.6% of those leaving in 1847/8. America was the preferred destination for these people, but a fare to Canada at £3 was a third of the cost and was attractive for this reason. In real terms, a fare to America could be had for less than the price of a heifer, or a summer's labouring in the fields.

Nearer to home, Glasgow became a destination for Ulster emigrants in particular. The huge numbers of destitute in the streets of Glasgow in 1849 became such a concern that the authorities began sending them back to Ireland, generally to Belfast, at a rate of one thousand per month. This exchange of the poor could have a local context. Three

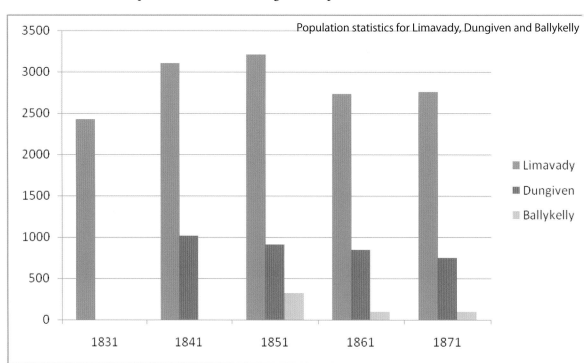

Donegal orphans were dispatched from Campsie to Glenties before being returned to Derry. From there they were sent to Glasgow with a few pence and a handful of biscuits. Limavady's population actually increased during the worst period of the Famine, although emigration was clearly an option since Alexander Given was operating a business as an Emigration Agent in Catherine Street in 1846.

The enormity of the problem that had faced the country should not be under-estimated. It was on a scale that would test the powers of modern governments to be able to respond effectively, even given their global resources, vastly improved communication systems, and well honed organisational skills. The Great Famine had several important and far-reaching consequences. By 1851, the population of the country had declined by two million on the previous figures of 1841. Almost one million had died and around one million had emigrated, and the decline continued. In 1900 there were barely four and a half million in Ireland. Much of this was due to changing patterns away from early marriage and land subdivision. Many landlords were anxious to sell off their land especially to clear their debts. From 1849 it became easier for them to do this, since at the same time tenants were realising the inherent problems in subdivision and stopped doing it. These factors combined to increase the number of larger holdings. Only one son could now inherit, if the farm was to be kept as a unit, and this would mean marrying later in life and waiting until the father died in order to do so. For the other sons and daughters, emigration became a solution to their problems. Resentment, against what they saw as the inaction of the English Government in dealing with the Famine, was carried in the minds of the Irish into later generations and to every country to which they emigrated. The landlord class too would be similarly condemned for their cruelty and inaction. In truth, while some landlords did little or nothing, and some exploited their position, there were those who did much to help and lost considerable sums of money in the process.

The British Government contributed less than half the cost of Famine Relief, the rest being raised from Ireland itself. Public works took £2.4 million alone and in 1853 the debts accrued by the workhouses were cancelled. Westminster contributed around £7 million overall and no European state had ever taken such vigorous action in coping with a disaster of this nature. This was the first time relief was organised on a national scale. However, the U.K.'s revenue was around £53 million in the 1840's, landlords continued to lift around 75% of their rents, and the Irish ports remained open. Just as governments do in the 21st century, the government of the day did not flinch at spending incredible sums on going to war. The Crimean War would cost £69.3 million. The danger of course in applying such hindsight, is that we impose a modern, different and therefore false set of values to a very specific context. With the best will in the world, we can only ever partially understand that context.

John Mitchel and The 1848 Revolutions

John Mitchel, from near Dungiven, did not see it that way at the time. In his fiercely partisan tract 'The Last Conquest of Ireland' he reflected on his years as a solicitor in Ulster. He wrote of evictions being signed, 'hundreds in one sheaf' in every county, and of 'whole neighbourhoods being thrown out upon the highways in winter.' The picture was more complex than that. Between 1846 and 1848 evictions in counties Armagh, Antrim and Monaghan seem to have been particularly relentless, but most landlords often demanded small sums in compensation rather than resort to legal

John Mitchel

ejectment. Knowing that they would be excluded from workhouse relief if they held a quarter of an acre or more many smallholders simply abandoned their plots during the Famine. Though not the period he refers to, Mitchel's description could be more accurately applied to the period after 1848, when forty-nine thousand families, or a quarter of a million persons throughout Ireland, were dispossessed in the post-Famine clearances. Ulster indeed does not seem to have suffered in these wholesale clearances as much as did the west and south-west. Many substantial tenants in Ulster had actually come through the harvest failures unscathed. When they eventually agitated in the 1850's along with southern Catholics, under the banner of tenants' rights, it was essentially to attempt to extend and legalise the unique 'Ulster Custom' that had long been accepted in the north by landlords. The basis of this 'Custom' was that it ensured there would be no eviction if the rent was paid and that if a tenant gave up his holding he could demand a lump-sum payment from the incoming tenant.

Mitchel would get heavily involved in the politics of protest. Charles Gavin Duffy, who had helped found the Young Ireland movement would employ him as a leading contributor on his newspaper The Nation. Duffy, like many others, had originally been inspired by the new ideas of racial and romantic nationalism that began to appear in Europe in 1842. When revolution flowed across Europe in 1848, Duffy would see it as the perfect opportunity for Ireland to liberate itself. Hunger was a major driving force behind this series of revolutions. After the first barricades went up in Palermo, most of Europe would be affected. King Louis Philippe was overthrown in Paris in February, and in March serious insurrections flared in Vienna, Budapest and Berlin.

Born in Scriggan Manse in Camnish near Dungiven in 1815, Mitchel was the son of the Reverend John Mitchel, a Presbyterian minister, and his wife Mary Haslett. His mother's brother William, was a banker in Derry and became Mayor of the city in 1843. The family moved to Derry in 1819 and then to Newry in 1823. A friend of his father's found Mitchel a place as a solicitor in Newry in 1836 and he married Jane Verner the year after, in Drumcree Parish Church.

After writing for The Nation from 1843, Mitchel was to become editor of the paper in 1847, until his strident views and militancy led to him resigning to set up his own paper, The United Irishman. It proved to be very popular, though it ran for only sixteen editions. Mitchel's spirit of protest surfaced during the Famine years when he remonstrated against the exportation of food from Ireland and his new paper advocated these views, calling for resistance and a policy of non-payment of rent. From the outset in February 1848, The United Irishman began appealing to the spirit of the 1798 Rebellion and urging an immediate mass uprising. The starving Irish though had no interest in insurrection. While government after government across Europe fell, the potential for a rising in Ireland was quickly and easily addressed.

On the 23rd May 1848, Mitchel was arrested with little difficulty. Tried by jury, he was sentenced to fourteen years 'transportation.' He was first sent to Ireland Island in Bermuda and then moved on to Tasmania where he arrived in April 1850 and where he would later be joined by his wife and family. It was while in enforced isolation on his way to Van Dieman's Land that he wrote his most important work, Jail Journal, the book which would secure his place in Irish nationalist history. In July 1853 Mitchel escaped to America where he again entered journalism. He began in New York by setting up a radical Irish nationalist paper called The Citizen, but resigned from this to tour the south of the country. When he was in the south he set up another paper, The Southern Citizen. He fought for the Confederate Army in the American Civil War and indeed lost two sons in that conflict. On the defeated side in the war, Mitchel was jailed briefly after it, on account of the articles he had penned both in support of Slavery and in support of the Southern States. He had justified Slavery by arguing that slaves were better fed and cared for than Irish cottiers. With the help of the Fenians organisation he was released from prison and once again launched a newspaper, which this time he called The Irish Citizen. The paper failed to attract readers and eventually folded, but Mitchel moved on to work for the Fenians for a time in Paris as a financial agent before returning again to America. When he eventually returned to Ireland in 1875, Mitchel would be elected M.P. for Co. Tipperary. His election was challenged however, on the grounds that he was

The statue of Mitchel in Newry

JOHN MITCHEL
1815 - 1875
AFTER TWENTY
SEVEN YEARS
IN EXILE FOR THE
SAKE OF IRELAND
HE RETURNED
WITH HONOUR
TO DIE AMONG HIS
OWN PEOPLE AND
HE RESTS WITH HIS
PARENTS IN THE 1st
PRESBYTERIAN OLD
MEETING HOUSE
GREEN AT NEWRY

a convicted felon and the situation was only resolved when Mitchel died later that same year. This then allowed the rival candidate to be selected unopposed. On his death in 1875, John Mitchel was buried in Newry and there is a statue to him in John Mitchel Place, just off the town's main street.

John Mitchel remains an important figure in Irish History because of his radical nationalist views. His writings, particularly his Jail Journal, would influence much of nationalist thinking in the years that followed and the 'boycott' adopted in many parts of Ireland to ostracize landowners, owes much to his ideas about 'passive protest.' The views he held always showed a high level of commitment. His writing on the Famine and Ireland castigates England, implying that the Famine was deliberate genocide, while his time in America found him giving his complete support to the Southern States and their ideas on the continuation of Slavery. Aidan Hegarty, in his book on John Mitchel, points out that on the two occasions that Mitchel was imprisoned, it was 'his ability with the pen and not the steel which landed him there.' Hegarty argues that while his writing had the capacity to provoke others, and at the same time often carried an implicit call to arms, it was writing itself that was John Mitchel's true vocation. He is remembered in several Gaelic Athletic Association Clubs like Newry's, Mitchel's G.F.C., and in Co. Derry's, John Mitchel's of Claudy. In his native town of Dungiven, Mitchel Park honours his name. On his voyage into exile, John Mitchel once recalled the natural beauty of familiar places. He wrote in his Jail Journal:

'my ear and my brain are filled with the murmurings of the
Rivers Roe and Bann.'

After involving himself in the unsuccessful campaign of the Irish Tenant League in the 1850's Mitchel's former employer, Charles Gavin Duffy emigrated to Australia. He became Prime Minister of Victoria in 1871 and was knighted in 1873. Ireland's contribution to the 'Year of Revolutions' was to be small in the scale of things. It would climax in July in the 'Battle of Widow McCormack's Cabbage Patch,' where a small police force, firing from a farmhouse in Co. Tipperary, dispersed fifty or so insurgents. During the summer of 1849, the revolutions in central Europe were finally put down and the dynastic powers regained their ascendancy once again. The nationalism that surfaced though would not go away forever. The zeal of the 1840's had awakened ancient ethnic passions. In the coming years it would democratise itself and become a major cause of the First World War. The rising ethnic rivalries in central and Eastern Europe had more in common with Ireland's apparently interminable sectarian tensions than is generally acknowledged. For some, British Imperialism would be a convenient focus for all of the country's ills, while for others it would be a convenient prop that could help ensure economic survival.

Ireland would have to wait a very long time before it had the maturity and the willingness to address its underlying problems and to be able to disentangle the fears and aspirations that bedevilled its own version of this rivalry.

William Makepeace Thackeray and Peg of Limavady

In 1842, the same year as the Workhouse was opening, the writer, historian and traveller, William Makepeace Thackeray passed through Limavady. Reputed to have been staying at the Mercer's Inn on Main Street, the thirty-one year old seems to have made his way to another inn, located on Ballyclose Street, for a drink. The blazing turf fire had a pot of potatoes on the boil when Thackeray was brought a beaker of ale by a maid with a "bewitching" smile that "lighted all the kitchen." Hardly able to take his eyes off her graceful movement, Thackeray spilt the ale causing her to burst into a peel of laughter. He was so smitten that he later put pen to paper to record the scene. In his poem about Peg, he describes her as "fair beyond compare" and when it featured in his Irish Sketch Book, the inn subsequently became known as the Peg of Limavady Inn.

The inn was eventually to become a bar known as Annie Quigley's. Though it is long gone, it is a pub which lives on in the folklore of many older residents of the town. The street was renovated beyond recognition in the

William Makepeace
Thackeray

Ballyclose Street (mid 20th century) with Annie Quigley's on the right

latter part of the 1900's and when an Old Peoples' Home was constructed on the site in 1976, it was appropriately named Thackeray Place. The writer had family connections in the locality. His uncle, the Reverend Elias Thackeray, had been Rector of Drumachose from 1807 to 1820 and it is known that William Makepeace stayed with relatives in Eglinton, after passing through Limavady. Thackeray actually says in his Sketch Book that he stayed little more than ten minutes in Limavady, implying that this was for a change of horses. Perhaps he lost all sense of time in the town, or perhaps this was just his use of poetic licence to further emphasise the impression Peg made on him. It has to be said however, that the number of words he finds to rhyme with Limavady, is proof enough that Thackeray really wanted to highlight the name of the town.

Peg of Limavaddy (extract)

Riding from Coleraine
Famed for lovely Kitty,
Came a Cockney bound
Unto Derry city.

This I do declare
Happy is the laddy
Who the heart can share
Of Peg of Limavaddy

Married if she were
Blest would be the daddy
Of the children fair
Of Peg of Limavaddy

Beauty is not rare
In the land of Paddy
Fair beyond compare
Is Peg of Limavaddy

Life in Limavady in the 19th Century

There would have been no shortage of alcohol available for Thackeray to try at the time, particularly in that area of town. During the 1800's Limavady witnessed a growth in the brewing and distilling trade which was, no doubt, helped by the increasingly plentiful supply of corn and barley in the area. Distilling was first recorded in Limavady in 1750 with John Alexander and Henry Small running rival distilleries. The Limavady innkeeper George Taylor was typical of the age. He operated a small, private, distilling business attached to his inn, around the same time as John Alexander and Henry Small. It was a precarious trade to be in and by the end of the century all three enterprises had ceased distilling, even as the brewing and distilling industry locally was starting to expand. David Cather began a large scale operation in about 1805 near Drumachose Church on Distillery Road or Church Street as it is now known.

When ownership of the Distillery Road business passed to Cather's son, George, he made the decision to lease the premises out. The new brewer, William K. Purcell took on the lease around 1850 and was soon advertising a wide range of products for sale. Purcell offered common beer, pale table beer, strong ale, double strong ale, strong porter and double strong porter, as well as pale India, or bitter ale and malt for bakers. Brewing

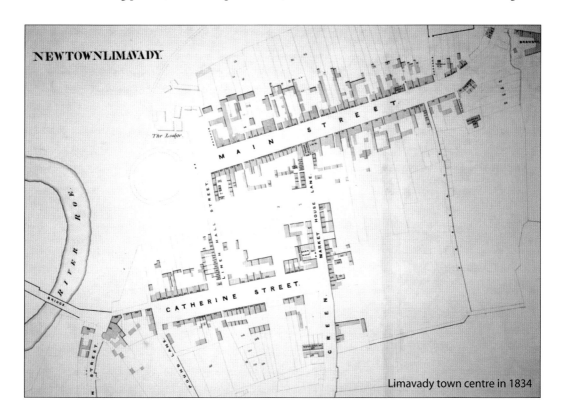

Limavady town centre in 1834

Church Street (formerly Distillery Road). The building behind the church may be the Distillery.

continued there after George sold out in 1864, though it changed owners at least twice before James Galloway and Company were described as 'brewers' at Ballyclose and Roe Mills, in 1870.

A decade later a Belfast firm, Young, King and Company converted George Cather's original brewery into a distillery. By 1883 the firm of distillers and blenders ran the Limavady Distillery, employing a Mr James McLoughlin on site as a Managing Partner. Mr Albert Bernard visited the Distillery Road site in the 1880's and provided a detailed description of the property. He tells us that the full estate covered ten acres, though the Distillery buildings only occupied about two acres. The premises were situated immediately beside Drumachose Church, separated only by a small alleyway.

The three bonded warehouses on Distillery Road contained 3,000 casks of Limavady Whisky of various ages. The company was known to export much of its product to wholesale houses in England, Scotland and 'the Colonies.'

On his tour of the premises, Bernard noted several Mash-tuns capable of containing 10,000 gallons each and a Worm-tub containing 20,000 gallons of water. Water for the Distillery came in a three mile long conduit from Well-Glass Springs and it seems almost inevitable then, that by 1895 there were complaints about a shortage of water getting to the Distillery. Having arrived by Northern Counties train and found the Distillery on a hill about ten minutes walk from the station, Bernard waxed lyrical about what he saw of the surrounding countryside - the rich vale of Myroe, the lofty splendour of Binevenagh and the roseate suffusion of autumn colours on Donald's Hill and Benbraddagh. He described how the clear and sparkling Well-Glass stream that supplied the Distillery was known as the Fairies' looking-glass and how it drew sprites

Limavady Distillery

to it, to arrange their tresses. Limavady whisky (nowadays spelt whiskey) was, he said, a well known product that cheered the heart and moistened the lips of many an Exile of Erin in distant colonies of the Empire. Once again however, the enterprise did not last and in 1914, Young, King and Company sold out to United Distillers, who subsequently closed everything down.

George Cather, the son of the original owner of the distillery, had other business interests in the area. He was the owner, for many years, of Carrichue Mills, on the outskirts of Ballykelly. The mill was recorded as being destroyed in a fire in 1884, but at one point a narrow gauge railway from these Indian and corn mills ran down to the main Limavady to Londonderry railway line.

As well as having started the brewing and distilling business in Distillery Road, George's father, David, had also operated a distillery on the Roemill Road, near the Hermitage, their family home. He had established this distillery in 1814 on the site of an earlier business dating from the 1700's. In 1835 it was being run by another son, William. Between November 1833 and April 1834 this site produced 21,000 gallons of whiskey, for home consumption. This must have included a Pure Malt, as an advertisement placed in the Chronicle by John Allen of Linenhall Street in November 1844, offered for sale, "10 puncheons" of William Cather's five year old Pure Malt Whiskey. Once again however the enterprise did not last and despite its apparent success, the premises were recorded as being disused by 1859.

Further on up the Roemill Road another distillery, connected to a corn mill, had been established in 1821 by William Moody. We know that in 1835, Moody set up machinery in the mill for the manufacture of pearl barley and that by 1846 it was being run very successfully by a Mr Peter Rankin. Leased in 1852 by Wiliam Carne and John Poulson, the distillery was noted for its potent malt whiskey. Once again though, just seven short years later it had ceased trading. James Galloway and Company, brewers and maltsters, of Distillery Road, revived it again in 1870, and ran it along with their existing operation.

Other types of business flourished at the time. The fine sharp sand in the neighbourhood would mean there would be many sandpits in operation and clay for brick making has always been readily available locally. In the 1800's brick kilns dotted the landscape. There were two sets of kilns at Ballykelly, a brickfield opposite Bessbrook and another kiln operating just west of the Rough Fort. Until relatively recent times a brick and tile works was operated by Irwin Douglas at Derrybeg, close to Derramore Presbyterian Church. Tiles were made near Aghanloo, and in Artikelly draining tiles were being manufactured in 1856. On Main Street, in the town itself, Andrew Given gave his trade as a brick and tile manufacturer in 1870.

A host of small businesses served the community in this period before the growth of mass production. In the last quarter of the 1800's, Stirlings, McCabes and Martins operated at various times as coach builders in the town and in Linenhall Street George Buchanan, and then Andrew Buchanan, worked as printers. For six shillings a year the residents could keep abreast of the world by purchasing The Limavady Journal and County Derry Advertiser which ran to four pages with six columns, though only the front page was printed locally. In 1887/88 a weekly paper called 'Brotherhood' was printed in Limavady by the Circle Co-operative Printing Company. It was the paper's intention, it said, to help 'the peaceful evolution of a happier and more just social order.' Printing of the paper was moved to Belfast in 1889 in anticipation of it being issued on a daily basis. This is presumably the same publication, though known as 'Limavady Brotherhood,' that Reverend Mullin cites in his history. Evolving into a monthly magazine and edited by J. B.Wallace, it ran on into 1918. There was sufficient demand for printing in Limavady in 1870 for Rebecca Buchanan and John Walker to be able to operate rival printing businesses in Linenhall Street and there was a bookbinder working out of premises in Irish Green Street. In 1846 neighbouring Londonderry had five bookshops while there was enough demand to keep four going in Coleraine. In that same year, out of nine smaller Ulster towns that had a population of between 3,000-4,000 inhabitants, most had only one bookshop, but Limavady, together with Larne and Dungannon managed to support three bookshops. From the early part of the century reading was increasingly seen as being important and this led to a growth in Reading Societies. Exactly 50% of

Limavady's Reading Society stock was made up of reading material that covered travel, geography, history and biography, while 22% was categorised as imaginative literature. It has to be remembered that these Societies tended to be drawn from the middle classes at this point. More generally, it is important to note that research into reading habits and reading tastes in the 19th and indeed the 18th century, clearly shows that people were not divided by religion when it came to what they chose to read. Literacy had penetrated into most parts of Ulster and had made an impact. The evidence would suggest that people in Ulster were no more immersed in a backward-looking oral tradition, than they were deeply versed in classical or biblical lore. It seems rather, that they were reading a broad range of printed literature that opened up a wider world to them.

Still a landmark to this day on Limavady's Main Street, The Alexander Arms, owned by Ann Wilson, was already an established hotel by 1824. On the Bessbrook River, Robert Wallace had a plating mill and forge, manufacturing spades and shovels, though he closed down the business in the summer months. Naves for cart wheels could be bought in Drumraighland from David Gresham and in later years Marshall's foundry at Crossnadonnell did casting work such as making cast-iron rollers. The Ross family in Ardmore did something similar, while small agricultural implements could be obtained from Elders of Derryduff or Whites of Camnish.

From the 1840's Hunters had a market in the town dealing in butter, pork and flax. This evolved into a corn milling business and later into the specialist bakery and coffee shop which operates on the site to this day. Where Main Street and Ballyclose Street met, on land which would adjoin the new railway station, the Macrory Mills operated as flour and corn mills from the end of the 1800's, until well into the 20th century.

Shirt making was becoming a major industry in Derry in the 1800's and in its infancy it used a system known as 'out-working.' This involved the running of various 'out-stations' in the towns and villages around Derry. Trained girls at the 'out-stations' would give out piece-work to local girls for them to complete the shirts as instructed. They would take this piece-work away to do it in their own homes. These instructions had to be followed strictly and when the finished garments were collected in, they were closely examined before payment was made. Wages for making the shirts ranged from 17½ pence per dozen and upwards. James Scott, of the city, placed an advertisement in the Londonderry Standard in 1851 stating that, given the rise in employment in the industry, he would be opening 'shirt-making establishments at or near Claudy, Donemana, Newton-Limavady and Moville.' In each place he was looking for a young woman capable of giving out and taking in the work and was also seeking young men aged sixteen to twenty to act as clerks. In the wider scale of things, from the 1850's on, a factory system was beginning to lead to the decline of the out-worker system, but nevertheless, as late as 1870, the shirt manufacturers McIntyre and Hogg and Company, opened premises in Catherine Street and Tillie and Henderson and Company opened premises in Linenhall Street. The decline was on its way and by 1912 the number of out-workers employed in the local industry had been cut by half. The total wage bill for people in country districts, which would have included Limavady, was still an impressive £40,000 at this stage. Perhaps it was the specialised nature of this work, piecing together the fronts, cuffs and neckbands, exclusively of white shirts, for the factories, that kept it viable for longer.

The town's economy was still very much centred on agriculture and as new farm machinery became available, a demonstration could attract a crowd. The local Kennaught Farming Society organised ploughing matches and cattle shows. In 1852 the Society organised that Mrs Gage's reaping machine would operate on a field of oats and wheat at Scroggy, owned by John Alexander. It coincided with the Cattle Show and the crowds were so great that they had trouble harnessing the three horses needed to pull the machine. The new reaping machine proved a success, taking off at such a speed that it needed thirty people going behind to lift and bind sheaves after it. There was such a throng though, that the wheat and oats in the field were soon in danger of being trampled underfoot and the demonstration had to be halted. A particularly impressive sight in 1877 too, would have been the traction engine S.M. Alexander of Roe Park had purchased in London. Drawing 'waggons' with thirty tons of manure, he used it to trundle between Limavady and his farm at Ballycairn near Coleraine at a leisurely four miles per hour.

The 19th century saw Limavady improve with the advances made in agriculture in the area. As the century progressed, there was not only enough corn being produced to meet the needs of the breweries and distilleries, but also enough for it to be exported through Derry. Wheat production also increased and a market had to be opened in the 1830's to dispose of the surplus flax being grown. In 1827 the growing trade prompted a proposal to construct a canal to carry produce directly from the town to the Foyle. Intended to run from Limavady to Ballymacran, the cost was calculated at £3,100. The plans drawn up by John Killaly included the construction of a pier at Ballymacran on the shores of the Foyle, where vessels could receive and discharge their cargo. A rail link to this pier was also proposed. It was envisioned that local grain could be exported using this link and that shells and shore manure along with imported slates, coal and timber, could be brought directly into the town using it. At a later stage the railway would eventually make its way into town, but nothing more was to come of the proposal

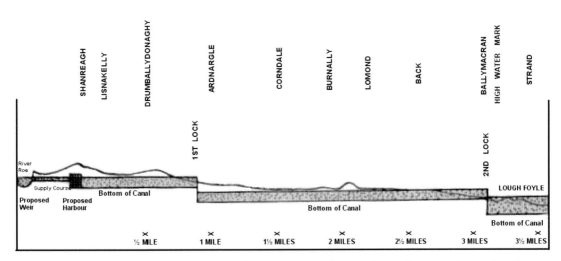

Section of the Proposed Canal from Newtonlimavady to Lough Foyle 1827

for the pier and the canal was never built.

Fairs and markets played an important part in the social calendar of our towns and villages, and these took place in the open air on the main streets. By the 1700's, in common with many other places, Dungiven was regularly holding two fairs in the year. Featuring cock-fighting, races and drinking, it seems that these 'fair' days managed to last the best part of a week. They continued to operate successfully into the 1800's in the town when another fair, held regularly on the second Tuesday of every month, was also added. Market day in Dungiven was, and still is, a Saturday. Two fairs were held in Ballykelly until 1807, but like the grain market set up in the village, these suffered from the increasing popularity of the fairs being held in neighbouring Limavady. At the other end of the borough, a meat and fur market was held on Benone Strand on Fridays. Although in its heyday this market attracted buyers from Belfast it was, no doubt, the drop in the public demand for rabbit skins and meat which led to its gradual disappearance.

Monday was traditionally the day the cattle market was held in Limavady, though butter, flax and potatoes were sold at this too. Cattle would indeed continue to be bought and sold on the town's streets until just before the start of the First World War. From 1820, Edward Boyle established grain markets on Tuesdays and Fridays in his specially erected 'large and commodious grain stores and shambles' in Market Street. An important horse fair was held on the second Monday in February with various other fairs held throughout the year on March 28th, June 13th, July 12th and on the 29th of

October. A glance at what was available at the Limavady fair of 1835 shows a wide variety of goods, animals and produce on offer. You could buy a book or a ballad, kitchen utensils, delph or hardware. Flax and linen were on sale as well as 'wearing apparel' and all the produce you would expect to find in a thriving country market, from eggs, butter, potatoes and meat, to cakes, fish, fruit, fowl, corn and meal. A young horse could be bought for between £6 and £15, with lambs going at 7 to 10 shillings each. Large oysters had become highly prized. There was a preference for the oysters from Greencastle which were considered to be 'large and of fine flavour' compared to those from the Myroe shore which were felt to be relatively small and insipid. During the 1830's fishermen from Magilligan parish netted between 400 and 500 oysters daily which they sold at '£3 per 31 hundred' to carriers, for sale in Newtownlimavady. The average labourer in the district though, earning up to 10d a day, would have to reflect a little before buying anything at all at the fair.

As well as serving as a marketplace for goods and commodities, the fairs sometimes served as a place where people could go to find work. By the late 19th century more than eighty towns in Ulster were holding these particular fairs known as Hiring Fairs. These fairs were normally held twice a year, on or around the 12th May and the 12th November as this coincided with times in the farming calendar when the work was heaviest and extra help was needed.

The largest Hiring Fairs in the west took place in Derry, Strabane, Omagh and Letterkenny and attracted hundreds of people from west Donegal. Limavady had its own Hiring Fair called the Gallop. Here men, women and children were hired on a six month 'term,' or in other words from one Hiring Fair to the next. Turning up in Limavady with a small 'bundle' under their arm, the man or woman, boy or girl, would make their way to the corner of Main Street and Market Street. The 'bundle' might contain some clothes or food, or perhaps even nothing at all, but it served as a signal that they were for hire. A person looking to be hired could expect to be looked up and down from head to toe, as the farmer weighed up how much work he could get out of the person. If he was hired, a man could hope to earn £6 a 'term' in wages, with lodgings and some food provided. When both parties were satisfied with the bargain the farmer took the man's 'bundle' and gave a shilling in return, sealing the contract. The man could then wander off to enjoy the rest of the day at the fair in the knowledge that he had found employment for the next six months. If boots, or other items, were needed to carry out the farm work, money was advanced by the farmer at the time and deducted at the end of the 'term.' With the coming of the 20th century, changing social conditions that were much accelerated by the First World War, meant 'day labour' became a more popular method of employing workers and the Hiring Fairs gradually disappeared. The last one held in Ireland is believed to have taken place in Milford, Co. Donegal, in 1947.

In 19th century Limavady and its wider locality, a family's diet would have been directly affected by its place in the social order. In summer the poor of the period, including cottiers and the poorer labourers, ate potatoes supplemented by milk and a stirabout made of oatmeal. In winter, potatoes and salt herrings were eaten. At Christmas, Easter and other festivals a small piece of bacon or meat was eaten to mark the occasion.

This was better, but not so far removed from the diet on offer in Newtownlimavady Workhouse in the 1840's, which consisted of four days of rice boiled with pork, seasoned with salt and pepper, and three days of wheaten bread with a quart of meat soup.

Moving up the social scale, the variety contained in the menu increased. Breakfast for farmers in the parish of Drumachose, could be either eggs, wheaten and oaten bread and butter with tea, or meal porridge, milk and potatoes. Dinner in Spring would have been smoked or salted beef, bacon, eggs and fowls. Lamb and fish would have been added to the diet in Summer and Autumn, while in the Winter months fresh beef, fish and rabbits were on the menu, with tea or porridge and potatoes and milk taken in the evening. Wealthy farmers in the parish of Banagher were able to have a side or two of good beef and two or three hams in the chimney and breakfasted on good stirabout and milk throughout the year. Homefed goose could feature on their tables, and on festive occasions oaten cake, butter and cheese were always present.

Doctors found themselves treating a great many patients who had digestive ailments. They characterised these ailments as indigestion, flatulence and dyspepsia. In the Ballykelly dispensary it was noted that almost every female above the age of thirty years was 'dyspeptic.' The local doctor claimed that it was the huge bulk of potatoes eaten that caused these gastric problems. An interesting comparison was made at the time between the ailments of a London alderman and an Irish peasant as it was noted that both suffered from the same gastric problem because of overloading the stomach. In the alderman's case it was a surfeit of rich delicacies, whereas for the Irishman it was an excess of the common potato. While we have to bear in mind the limited ability of Medicine to diagnose and treat illness at the time nevertheless, dispensaries from Garvagh to Newtownlimavady were treating more cases of digestive disorder than of any other ailment.

An analysis of the diets of the labouring classes in Ireland in the 1830's however, showed that those living in the county of Londonderry had greater variety in their diet, than those living in many other areas. Their diet was slightly more varied than those living in Antrim and Down for example and it was considerably more varied than that of the labouring classes living in the west or the centre of Ireland, in Cavan, Donegal or Monaghan.

In the second half of the 19th century there were noticeable changes to the diets of the average Irish labourer in the county. While pork and meat were still luxuries, Indian meal, flour, bread, tea and sugar were regularly being consumed in addition to potatoes, milk, buttermilk, oatmeal and herring. For those who had survived the Famine and were now experiencing a rise in their living standards, the potato played a less dominant role in their diet. In terms of its nutritional value however, this greater variety was actually less nutritious. In short, the labourers' less varied diet of 1836 was generally better than the more varied diet they are recorded as eating in 1859.

While communities could attempt to bring organisation, order and an air of progress to their everyday existence in the 19th century, they were still confronted by sudden outbreaks of illness and disease. Near the entrance to Christ Church grounds a prominent monument holds the mass grave of the victims of a cholera outbreak that swept the town in 1832. A Cholera Hospital operated in the period and, despite the 'promptness of the measures taken' and the 'excellence of the physician,' the outbreak saw three hundred cases and thirty deaths, in ten days. In one day there were seventy-three new cases in the Ballyclose area. The writer of the O.S. Memoirs noted, tellingly, that the town had never been 'cleansed.'

Even in the midst of the Famine, in 1846, life still had to go on and we find the decision being taken in that year, to use boards to name the houses and streets in the town. Within two years fresh water would be "piped" into Limavady, as

The mass grave of the cholera victims

opposed to arriving in a water course, as it had done until then. The threat of disease would continue however and in 1854 Sanitary Officers began a two year campaign of cleaning up the town's streets and houses. They removed dunghills from Irish Green Street and sorted out unfit drains from behind the meeting house area.

Fighting the spread of disease was a never-ending battle however and that same year, in neighbouring Ballykelly, there were new cases of diphtheria and typhos. Huge advances in sanitation, combined with medical discoveries, would eventually bring major and universal improvements to peoples' health and welfare, but all this was a long way away and would not be felt until well into the next century.

In a world much different from the present day, fast, efficient and reliable communication systems were only slowly developing. The use of the new electric telegraph meant that from 1852, The Belfast News Letter was able to get much quicker and more ready access to news from outside Ulster. While newspapers in this era regularly recorded and commented on political events from around the world, they also carried advertisements promoting all manner of services to their local public. In 1844, The Coleraine Chronicle carried a notice stating that from Monday 27th May, the Tobermore/Dungiven Car would be leaving Dungiven at 8 a.m. and returning at 2.30 p.m. the same day. The Car could take four passengers and potential customers were informed that it would link up with the Mail Cars for other places. It would cost 1shilling and 6 pence for a single journey and 2 shillings and 6 pence for a return journey.

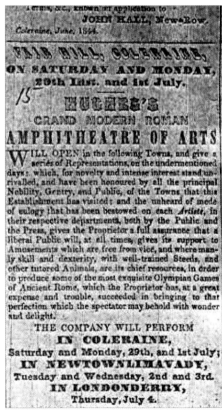

Limavady would certainly have been the place to be on Tuesday 2nd and Wednesday 3rd July 1844. The town was to be visited by Hughes's Grand Modern Roman Amphitheatre of Arts. A magnificent pavilion, capable of holding 2,000 spectators, was to be erected 'in the space of 3 hours' to host the show. Mr Hughes himself would perform the incredible feat of driving fourteen pairs of horses at one time in procession and a 'colossal' performing elephant from Ceylon was coming to Limavady with the show. Performances on both nights would be at 7 o'clock

Hughes's Amphitheatre visits
Newtownlimavady

and a show, taking place at 2 o'clock, would be 'purposely arranged for the convenience of the families of the Nobility and Gentry who cannot attend in the evening.'

It was through an advertisement in the Chronicle that local gentry were reminded that J. Smyth, tea dealer and draper in the town, was the sole agent for Howqua's and Mowqua's celebrated teas. Since a consignment of these quality teas had recently become available at a reduced price, it was felt that this might interest the 'serious tea drinkers' in the area.

Even horses made the papers. The owner of Musquito, a dark chestnut stallion standing sixteen hands high, advertised in the Chronicle that the horse would be available all season at Downhill to cover mares.

A little later in the period, The Londonderry Sentinel carried news of an unusual auction. It was to take place on the 5th of February 1878 at noon on Magilligan Strand. 'Sails, spars, water casks and other wreckage now lying on the beach' were to be sold. Everything going under the hammer was material salvaged from the wreck of the Norwegian Brig, Hilding.

The ship, had floundered on the 25th January 1878 at the mouth of the Foyle on the tuns, or sand banks, when attempting to find shelter from a ferocious storm. The plight of the crew had been spotted by the Reverend Thomas McClelland in Greencastle, acting on behalf of the local Coastguard. The terrible sea conditions meant the lifeboat was unable to effect a rescue. Two of the crew, Captain Jargenson and P. Bertingers, both originally from Norway, were drowned when they set off to swim ashore to raise the alarm. Fellow Norwegian, Karl Sucke, was washed overboard while in the process of climbing the rigging. At first light on Saturday 26th January, using George Leeke's 'cobble' fishing boat, seven local fishermen from Magilligan, led by Master Mariner James McCandless, together with his brother Samuel, attempted to rescue those who remained on board. Those involved in the rescue mission were the two McCandless brothers, George Leeke himself, Michael Rodden, Samuel McCorriston, John Deeney, James Cramsie and George Dougan. Against all the odds, they managed to save the four crew still remaining on the ship. Two of the men saved, Franz Norman and Antonia Kithna, were Dutch. The other two rescued were Peter Anderson from Norway, and sixteen-year-old Donald McDonald from Ontario, Canada. Erich Henrichsen and Johans Matthiessen, both from Finland, were also rescued, but they were brought to safety from near the shoreline, having been washed in towards the coast clinging to a 'spar.' A Coroner's Inquest was held on Monday 28th January in Mr Lafferty's Public House, Benone, which is now known as Cooley's. The three sailors who drowned were buried on 31st January, in Tamlaghtard Parish Church, though only the name of Captain

Jargenson is recorded with a headstone in the graveyard. A great sense of gratitude was felt by many at the time and donations were raised to thank all the men involved, as well as Mrs Henry Sherrard and Lady Bruce, two ladies who had kindly opened their homes to the rescued sailors. Details of the tragic tale were unearthed in 2008/9 by local historian and Treasurer of the Roe Valley Historical Society, Robert Guthrie. His discovery captured wider interest in the sad and long forgotten circumstances of the affair and, with the support of the Norwegian Consul, local schoolchildren and Limavady Borough Council, an annual commemoration is set to mark the event each January at the graveside of Captain Jargenson.

It was really only the storm which had brought the Hilding to Ireland. The Brig had left Glasgow on Friday the 10th January bound for Cardenas in Cuba, with a cargo of coal. Encountering some difficulty with the weather, from the outset, the captain had made the decision to shelter in the Clyde up until the 13th January, before continuing the journey. The rescue drew, not only a lot of sympathy locally, but also, a great deal of attention in the local papers. The Norwegian government too got to hear of the rescue and expressed its gratitude to James McCandless, presenting him with 'a binocular' some time afterwards. The auction on the strand, of the 'materials saved from the wreck,' had offered the ship's cargo of coal for sale. This amounted to 248 tons of best steam coal and 159 tons of gas coal. The only drawback for any purchaser was that it was 'on board said vessel as she now lies.' We don't know if anyone bid for the coal at the auction, but it is said lumps of it were occasionally washed up onto the Magilligan shore in the years that followed.

Locally, Samuel Stirling would almost certainly have been aware of this big news story at the time. He was born on 15th May 1838 and by 1879 was a Town Commissioner in Limavady. He went on to hold the position of Urban Councillor from 1898 to 1907 and he is especially noteworthy because a fountain, now located on Main Street, was 'placed here in his memory' in 1909. The fountain has been moved up and down the street in the course of the last thirty or forty years, but Samuel's life must have had a particular impact at the time to have had the fountain dedicated to him. The tribute on the fountain gives tantalising clues about his character, describing him as 'a man who loved Limavady and always tried to promote its interests. His kindness of heart and honesty of purpose, gained him the affectionate esteem of all who knew him.' Samuel Stirling's lifetime also coincided with a genuine highpoint in the town's achievements on the sports field.

Sport has long played an important part in the recreational life of Limavady people. The present day Limavady United Football Club, for example, claims its origins go back to a football side formed in 1876 in Limavady. Certainly the sport must have been strong in this era, locally. On the 18th November 1880, in the Queen's Hotel, Belfast, a club from Limavady called 'Alexander' was one of the seven founder members that met and formed the Irish Football Association. 'Alexander' also contributed, at that time, to the purchase of the original Irish Cup. The side's name crops up again in February 1884 when 'Alexander' played a match against another local club, 'Limavady Wanderers.' The two teams amalgamated in that same year to become Limavady United, and it was under this name that they went on to reach consecutive Irish Cup Finals in 1885 and 1886. Meeting Distillery in both finals, United lost the first final, three nil and the second final, one nil. Variously known as 'The Lims,' or 'The Roesiders,' it would be 2004/5, well over a century later, before the club would manage to reach even the semi-final of another Irish Cup. The club's prowess throughout the period is clearly evident though, as it provided several internationals to the Irish national side of that era. James Rankin was capped in 1882/83, Tom McLean in 1884/85, Joe Sherrard in 1884-88, Oliver Devine in 1885-88, James Allen and Nathaniel Brown in 1886/87 and George Forbes in 1887/88. Limavady United proved they could hold their own with the best of them by travelling to Liverpool in 1886 and defeating the famous English side, Everton Football Club, by one goal to nil. Joe Sherrard struck the goal that day in a team that included fellow internationals J. Allen, W. Douglas, and W.M. Browne. A photograph of this legendary side took pride of place in Andy and Johnny McCaughey's barber's shop on Main Street, where it remained, until the shop closed some time late in the 20th century. Andy McCaughey had a long association with the club, both as a supporter and as an administrator. It is not clear if Nathaniel Browne and W. M. Browne, are one and the same person, but even if we assume they are, it means Limavady produced no less than eight international players in this era. The town is unlikely ever to repeat this achievement, but it has continued to produce players of exceptional talent right through to the modern age, in the likes of Eric McManus, Michael Guy, and most notably of course, the highly gifted Irish International Gerry Mullan. Significantly too, a local man, steeped in the tradition of the game in the area, Raymond Kennedy, is currently the President of the Irish Football Association.

Having learned to swim in the Roe, James McCallion of Limavady won the Irish Mile Swim from Berrin Rock to Portstewart quay, in July 1865, while at the same event another McCallion won the junior race. Many such pastimes and sports have played a major part in the popular culture in the area for a great many years, from boxing and greyhound racing, to fishing, darts, and horseshoe throwing. Like Gaelic games however, despite having a strong tradition, these pastimes are often poorly documented. It would not be until 1903, for example, that we hear of a hurling team being established locally as St Patrick's Hurling Club. The club had immediate success, producing Henry Patton, who won an Ulster medal with Derry in the Ulster Senior Hurling Championship Final in that same year. In a later era, in Gaelic Football, Harry Owens would captain the Derry team of the 1930's and 1940's, and would also represent Ulster.

Cricket, on the other hand, is well documented. For the moment, cricket matches in the area can be traced further back in time, than any of the other major sports. An organised game was played in 1855, at the Chapel Lane, on the Cricket Field owned by Major Alexander Boyle J.P, a local dignitary. The club was known as Newtown Limavady Cricket Club until 1864, when it changed its name for a year to West End Cricket Club. The following year it adopted the name Limavady Cricket Club and an annual fixture was organised against Drenagh Estate. Other matches were played against Pellipar, Cumber, Foyle College, Feeny, Castlerock, and Greencastle in Donegal. The Limavady Brass Band, under Andrew Given, attended matches and an invariable part of the day's programme was a 'sumptious luncheon.' Matches were not confined to local teams however and on Friday 7th July 1865 the Scottish club, Greenock, visited Limavady. They were the guests of Mr W.S. Ross of Barley Park House on Irish Green Street and the match was played at Deerpark. The Limavady openers were C.T. McCausland and J. Alexander, but Greenock proved too strong for the local side and the visitors went on to win by eight wickets. Showing great enterprise though, Limavady gained the services of a professional coach, and provided three players for the County Derry side that played County Donegal in 1870, in Letterkenny. In 1888, Limavady became the first winners of the North West Senior Cup in an era that must have seemed like a golden age for sport, given the success of cricket and soccer locally at the time. A golden age perhaps, though in 1895 the Ballymoney Free Press sensed the world was on the brink of change when it wrote that while the bicycle was fast superseding the horse for riding purposes, 'the horseless carriage is destined to succeed both.' The intensity of that change would surprise everyone as the Great War cut through the male population of Ireland's cities, towns and villages. Around Limavady, as elsewhere, there would be no clearer manifestation of this, than the petering out of these sporting clubs. They would have to remain dormant until men returned from war to breathe new life into them.

The Londonderry Air and Danny Boy

In relatively recent times, The Londonderry Air has become a cultural symbol of Ireland. While the written notation of the tune can be traced back to the 1850's, its

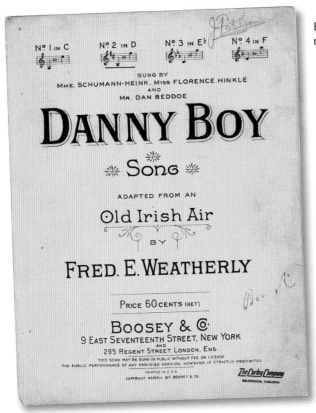

Boosey & Co. published the notation in the USA.

all-conquering popularity seems to have been assured only after the Englishman Fred Weatherly published his words in 1912, to make it 'Danny Boy'. Weatherly, who was a solicitor by profession, was also a prolific writer of books and lyrics. He had originally written a song called Danny Boy in 1910, the same year in which he had lost both his father and his son. Weatherly was still not satisfied with the song and re-wrote it a year later in 1911. When his sister-in-law sent him a Manuscript of a new tune from America that she had heard sung by miners in Colorado, Weatherly quickly adapted this set of lyrics once again. This time it was "to make it fit that beautiful melody." Weatherly later discovered that his friend Alfred Perceval Graves had already written two sets of words to the tune. Believing that the melody demanded "a human interest" that was lacking in these two versions, he wrote to Graves to explain his thinking. The Irish born poet and songwriter Alfred Perceval Graves had been responsible for publishing a great many Irish songs and ballads. It is perhaps not that surprising then that Weatherly was to find his old friend "did not take my explanation in the spirit which I hoped."

Several attempts have been made over the years to write lyrics to the haunting tune,

Fred Weatherly

but the combination of words and sentiments penned by Weatherly and eventually published by Boosey in 1913 have stood the test of time, like no others before or since.

Jane Ross (1810-1879), who lived on Main Street Limavady, is acknowledged as the person who originally brought the air to a wider audience in the 1850's. The

Society for the Preservation and Publication of the
Melodies of Ireland had been inviting people to send
it copies of Irish music and songs for publication. Jane,
it seems, forwarded this tune to Mr George Petrie, the
Society's President. A book was eventually published
in 1855 in which the air was listed as a song, under the
category 'Anonymous Airs.' It would not be given the
title 'The Londonderry Air' until it appeared as that in
an 'Irish Song Book' edited by A. P. Graves, in 1894.
The title may have been nothing more than a simplistic
geographical convenience at the time, but it continues

Jane Ross

to do Limavady a mild disservice in that it acknowledges the county, rather the town,
of its origin.

Jane Ross was one of four unmarried daughters of Mr John Ross, a former provost of
Limavady. A plaque marks the house where she lived on the town's Main Street and her
grave and headstone are to be found in Christ Church cemetery. How exactly the tune
came into the possession of Jane Ross is another question. Lots of suggestions have been
made. It has been said that she may have heard it from a well-
known local fiddler, Blind Jimmy McCurry. Another claim says
it had been composed originally as 'O'Cahan's Lament' by one
of Donal Ballagh's musicians to mourn the loss of his lands. Yet
another claim holds that it was by Rory Dall, the blind harper,
who also composed it as a lament for the loss of his lands. It
has also been said that O'Hempsey, the celebrated blind harper
from Magilligan, was the one who wrote it. On the other hand
it has been pointed out that one of the unique features of the
tune, as we have it from Jane Ross's time, is that it does not fit
a traditional Irish ballad metre. Nor indeed does there seem to
have been variations of the tune in circulation as would normally
be the case with a traditional air. Anyone who has tried to sing it
will know that part of the tune has an unusually high pitch. It is
said that this gives it a wider range than was normal to find sung
at Ireland's firesides, or in her streets and lanes. The mystery
is further compounded by the fact that Jane Ross is known to
have written her own tunes, at least a couple of which have
been preserved. There is speculation that what she forwarded

The plaque on the house in Main
Street where Jane Ross lived

The Ross family grave

to Petrie may have been her own original piece based on an Irish theme. All this recent speculation seems only to be fired by the immense and unending popularity of the song.

What is certain though, is, that Jane Ross allowed the tune to emerge to public acclaim from her home in Limavady, early in the 19th century. The words by Weatherly took the air to a new level of popularity at a time when Europe, thanks to the First World War, was witnessing a degree of sorrow and loss that would scarcely be equalled, ever again.

Danny Boy has been recorded by just about every artist who ever sang. Tony Bennett, Johnny Cash, Roy Orbison, Bing Crosby, Cliff Richard, Cher and Elvis have all recorded the song. Indeed it is said it was a favourite of The King's and that it was played at his funeral. The song's popularity sees little sign of waning. In March 2008 a fifty hour long Danny Boy Marathon held in Michigan managed to attract over 1,000 performers. The artists sang it in Polish, French, English and Yiddish and it was done in American Sign and 'rap' and was played on every instrument from a harp to a kazoo. The 'Danny Boy' name is now used commercially to market whiskey and a range of merchandise from souvenirs to sweatshirts. By these standards, our local Danny Boy Festival has more to do to fully capitalise on the enormous worldwide potential interest that exists in the song. Weatherly's original words were:

Oh Danny Boy, the pipes, the pipes are calling
From glen to glen, and down the mountain side.
The summer's gone, and all the roses falling,
It's you, it's you must go and I must bide.
But come ye back when summer's in the meadow,
Or when the valley's hushed and white with snow,
It's I'll be here in sunshine or in shadow,-
Oh, Danny Boy, O Danny Boy, I love you so!

But when ye come, and all the flowers are dying,
If I am dead, as dead I well may be,
Ye'll come and find the place where I am lying,
And kneel and say an Ave there for me.
And I shall hear, though soft you tread above me,
And all my grave will warmer, sweeter be,
For you will bend and tell me that you love me,
And I shall sleep in peace until you come to me!

The Railway comes to Limavady

In 1845 Parliament authorised the building of a railway from Londonderry to Coleraine, with a branch line to Limavady. This required the making of embankments along Lough Foyle and the reclaiming of a considerable amount of land. Powers had already been granted in 1838 to embank the slob lands from the mouth of the Faughan to Magilligan Point and the plan was to reclaim up to 25,000 acres. With the cost running to £50,000 for the first 4,000 acres the project would end up being less ambitious, but nonetheless impressive. The Ballykelly reclamations were completed between 1838 and 1845 and in October 1845 a contract was signed with the railway company to make the Foyle embankment and the Downhill tunnels. The company intended to reclaim up to 20,000 acres and sell it off to pay for their costs, but in the end it seems they reclaimed only around 900 acres.

The Londonderry to Coleraine line's first train into Coleraine arrived on Friday 22nd July 1853 and was welcomed with suitable occasion and ceremony. Coleraine was decorated and as well as a meal, comprising 'every luxury of the season,' a trip for three hundred of the principal subscribers and inhabitants was organised to Downhill and Magilligan. The new line into Limavady had opened before this however, at the beginning of October 1852. It branched off from the main line at Limavady Junction in Myroe and ran for about three and a quarter miles to Limavady town. Prior to this, the transport links with Londonderry and Coleraine would have been by coach, which was both slow and relatively uncomfortable. With the coming of the railway, the excitement at the time must surely have been tangible. The introduction of the railways to the country was of course not without its objectors. A few years earlier in Belfast, the railways would be condemned for just about every reason conceivable. It was claimed their smoke would frighten cows and prevent them from producing milk. The Belfast Presbytery condemned the running of trains on the Sabbath and one minister told his congregation that trains were transporting "souls to the devil at the rate of 6d a piece." He went on to claim that every blast of a railway whistle was "answered by a shout in Hell."

Limavady though, like Coleraine, seems to have welcomed the railway's arrival. For the opening, a special train carrying the nobility and gentry ran from Londonderry. On its arrival, a brass band was organised to lead the guests up Limavady's Main Street to a banquet in the Town Hall. Unfortunately when the train pulled in, there were a few red faces when it was discovered that the new platform had been built too high and that it was impossible to open the doors of the train. The elegantly dressed party had to

The former Magilligan Station

clamber out awkwardly on the opposite side.

Passenger trains officially began running on 29th December that same year and almost immediately there was a regular traffic of Derry merchants coming by train to Limavady to buy grain. Flax buyers too, seemed to be keen to use the very newest form of transport. In October 1854, they petitioned to have the flax market opened a little later in the day so that they could catch the morning train and still be on time.

The following summer, in 1855, a three mile branch line was opened between Magilligan station and Magilligan Point which connected with a steamer service to Innishowen. The Point soon boasted a fine hotel, latterly known as Leek's Hotel.

An intermediate station existed at Drummond providing four trains a day in each direction. With a journey time of forty minutes this was most probably a horse drawn train and the branch closed after a few months, having quickly proved uneconomic. Traces of the branch line can still be found in the area.

The premises for Limavady's new station were not to follow immediately. These were only built in 1874 after The Northern Counties Committee had taken over the Londonderry and Coleraine Railway. Designed by the railway architect John Lanyon, they were built in variegated red brick. With John's famous father, Charles Lanyon holding the office of Chairman of the Northern Counties Railway from 1870 to 1887, it was not perhaps that surprising. As well as designing our former railway station, John Lanyon designed many of Castlerock's important buildings and he was also responsible for supervising the much needed restoration of Downhill Palace, between 1870 and 1874. The railway expansion in the area continued in 1878 when an Act authorised the extension of the line to Dungiven.

The Point Bar (left), Fisherman's Hut (centre) with Leek's Hotel (right)

The newly formed Limavady and Dungiven Railway Company met at the Limavady terminus in March 1880 with Samuel Maxwell in the chair. The railway was promoted with a capital of £100,000, made up of 7,500 shares of £10 each. The Board of Works invested £25,000 and a further £20,000 came from the Skinners Company, whose lands centred on Dungiven. The Skinners saw the railway as key to the town's future prosperity and had gone as far as to guarantee 5% interest on the shares.

Railway Place and Passengers' Entrance to the Station

Mr Langridge, master of the Skinners Company, turned the first sod at Dungiven in May 1880. The line opened in July 1883 and was linked to the existing branch at Limavady by passing it through a bridge at Lower Main Street. Intermediary stations were set up on the line to Dungiven at Ardmore, Derryork and Drumsurn. The Ardmore station was built at the insistence of S.M. Macrory, who had his house, land and mills nearby. He granted the Railway Company right of way through his land in exchange for the Halt. In Drumsurn the corn mills, flax mills, lime works and quarries would provide a variety of goods that could be exported by rail. Already running a thriving general merchant's store, O'Connors would expand their business to offer hotel accommodation during the building of the line. In order to get its burnt limestone to the railway, Kilhoyle Lime Works in the area used a tramway system to carry it to the Gortnarney Road. A weighted buggy heading down to the road brought an empty one back up to be filled. From there, a horse and cart would then take the load to the railway station. Lime was a valuable commodity commonly used as fertiliser to reduce soil acidity and also for lime mortar in building work.

The grand inauguration of this branch line fared little better than the original one to Limavady. Open carriages were used on the train and by the time the visiting guests arrived in Dungiven, the fine white dresses of the ladies on board were covered in engine soot. While the investors may have had high hopes that the line would exploit the sandstone beds and

Railway routes in our area

Limavady Railway Station platform

the iron ore of Benbraddagh, in the long term, the line was never a success and never made money. The independent Limavady and Dungiven Railway Company went out of existence in 1907. The Northern Counties Committee, who had hired the company its rolling stock, bought the ten miles of track, four stations, sidings, signals and goods yards, for £2,000. The N.C.C. could not make the line pay either and passenger services ended in 1933, with goods services stopping a few years later. The line was used by the armed forces during the Second World War but closed definitively in 1950, with the line from Limavady to Limavady Junction in Myroe closing in 1955. The station buildings and sheds in Limavady, together with the railway bridge at Lower Main Street, formed a major and extensive landmark at the bottom of the town. The bridge was demolished in May 1964 during a road improvement scheme. Parts of the station were used as a bus depot for the Ulster Transport Authority for many years, but the station itself fell into disrepair and it too was eventually demolished in October 1974. Some time later the remaining goods sheds were replaced by a modern, cream brick, purpose-built, Bus Depot. Several of the pillars prominent in the photograph of the station platform, were used to good effect in the construction of a bus shelter erected on Catherine Street in the latter part of the 20th century.

J.E. Ritter and the Hydroelectric Power Station

The end of the 1800's was a period of great hope and expectation across the western world. A glut of new ideas and inventions quickly transformed the lives of ordinary people at this time, and none more so than the discovery and mastery of electricity for lighting and heating.

Electricity made such an impact at the Paris trade exhibition of 1900, that Paris would subsequently become known throughout the world as 'The City of Light.' Although Faraday had invented the electric motor and generator as far back as 1821, it took some time for the potential to be realised commercially. The city of London had in fact

introduced the first electric street lighting in 1878, in advance
of the Paris exhibition, and in that same year Cragside House,
a large private house in Northumberland, was lit by electricity.
Armstrong, the owner of Cragside, was a wealthy inventor,
armaments manufacturer and a keen amateur engineer. His
pioneering work at his home in Cragside used an artificial
lake dug out on his property to create the hydro-electricity
that lit his home.

J.E. Ritter

Cragside is held to be the first private house in Britain lit
by electricity but the curator of Milford House in Co. Armagh
claims that the wealthy industrialist, R.G. Mc Crum, had installed hydro-electricity in
1870 in Milford House, some eight years before Cragside. The McCrum family had been
one of Ireland's foremost linen manufacturers and Robert created the model village of
Milford. McCrum's innovations at Milford House would make it the earliest private
house in Great Britain and Ireland to have had electricity.

Initially of course, it would be something that only the wealthy could afford to have
installed. The Traill brothers of Bushmills were in this category and had developed an
intense interest in this new technology. Their passion led them to set up the world's
first ever hydro-electric tramway at Bushmills. The tramway was originally designed
to carry goods, but the tourist potential was quickly spotted and a passenger service,
running from Portrush to Bushmills, was officially launched on 28th September 1883.
With the scenic coastal route proving popular, the line was extended to include the
Giant's Causeway, which had already become a much visited tourist attraction.

An exhibition of 'lighting by electricity' organised by the Northern Constitution
in 1889 in its New Row premises in Coleraine, stimulated further interest in the new
technology in the north-west. Impressed by the Maxim-Western Electric Lighting
Company's operations, Mr James Bellas set up electric lighting in his timber yard at
Beresford Place. At the same time Mr William Ellis installed a dynamo driven by a
steam engine for lighting his premises and offices in the Diamond.

For the amateur engineer and wealthy landowner John Edward Ritter, living in
nearby Limavady, the temptation must have been too much. Shortly afterwards he
began to experiment with electricity around his house and its out-buildings. In the early
1890's he installed a Hornsby-Ackroyd oil engine in the farmyard attached to his home,
Roe Park House, now the Radisson Roe Park Hotel.

Using a series of belts and pulleys this small paraffin fuelled engine drove a chaff
cutter, a turnip cutter and a saw bench. In 1893 Ritter decided to extend the experiment

by introducing electric lighting to Roe Park House itself and to some of its out-buildings. For this purpose he obtained a direct current electric generator or 'dynamo' manufactured by W.H. Allen. This was then driven by the existing oil engine via a belt and pulley system. The engine was used to drive the 'dynamo' from early morning until daylight and from dusk until bedtime, depending on the seasons. With this successfully operating, Ritter now turned to the potential offered by the river which ran through his land. In 1895 he purchased a second direct current electric generator. This time he linked it to a water wheel at his Largy Green saw mills. After their marriage in 1887, Ritter and his wife had inherited the sawmills as part of their extensive estate on the west bank of the river.

In 1896, the year after purchasing the direct current generator, Ritter and his wife built a hydro-electric power station at the Largy Green, in the present day Roe Valley Country Park. At the same time an existing overhead line from the Largy Green to Roe Park House was fitted with oil filled insulators, to make it suitable for single phase alternating current at 1100 volts. The line was continued into Limavady, and substations were built to transform the voltage to the 220/110 three wire, required for distribution to houses.

One of the £10 Gas Shares issued at the time

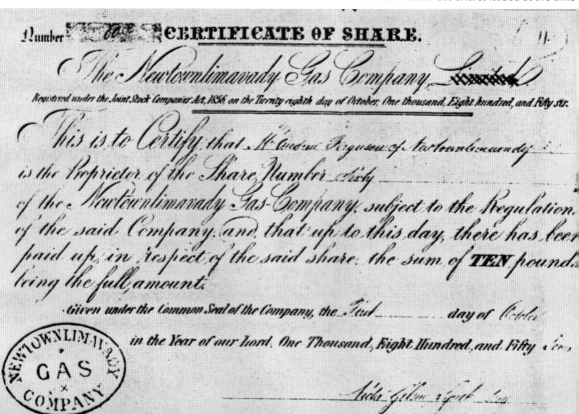

The route of the new line went through Ritter's Roe Park demesne until it reached the south side of the Roe Bridge and the town boundary. It was then taken under a dry arch out to the north side of the river where it continued on private property to The Lodge. The first substation in the town was a small wooden building, eight feet by six feet near the entrance to The Lodge. It was situated just behind the house's former gate lodge, a local landmark for many years at the top of Main Street that was known as the Inkpot. Another substation was placed at the rear of the Alexander Arms Hotel on Main Street, this time in a small brick building. The line itself went across the garden and farmyard of The Lodge to the 'back walks,' a private walled path that ran from The Lodge to an orchard near Christ Church cemetery.

Ritter had intended erecting low-voltage overhead distribution lines on wooden poles in the four main streets of the town, but the Town Council refused him permission to place these on public property. There were other interests at work. From the outset, the Limavady Gas Company had opposed the introduction of electricity into the town as it threatened their monopoly of the heating and lighting market. At one point, the Town Council had hoped to purchase the Gas Company and make it a municipal concern. A bitter and long-fought dispute would soon develop between Ritter and the Gas Company. Formed in 1852, with the intention of providing gas lighting, shares in the Gas Company sold rapidly at £10 each and the Company had installed itself in premises on present-day Connell Street.

The Gas Company was long established before Ritter came on the scene and as far back as 1855 it was lighting the town with thirty gas lamps. The Company's contract required it to light the lamps an hour after sunset, extinguish fifteen of them at 11p.m. and leave the remaining fifteen lit until an hour before sunrise. None were to be lit on clear moonlit nights. The lanterns and posts were the town's responsibility, while the lighting and extinguishing of the lamps fell to the Gas Company.

It was in June 1897 that Ritter had applied to the Board of Trade for a Provisional Order licence, to allow him to supply electricity in accordance with the Electric Lighting Acts. He needed the Order if he was to challenge the Council and the Gas Company, but he was determined to find other ways to advance his project as he waited for this to come through. He set about making arrangements with various land and property owners in town who allowed him to erect distribution lines at the rear of their homes and premises. That way he only had to cross the main streets at two places, one underground and one high overhead.

The first customers to be connected to the new electric lighting were Miss Lancey, who lived in The Lodge, and Tom Moore, a confectioner and greengrocer in Linenhall

ELECTRIC LIGHT AND POWER STATION,

Largy Mills,

Limavady, June, 1897.

Having applied for a licence or Provisional Order under the Electric Lighting Acts of 1882 and 1888, the charge fixed for Electric energy in the Model Order of the Board of Trade is per quarter : For any amount up to twenty units, thirteen shillings and fourpence, and for each unit over twenty units, eightpence.

I am however, willing to supply current by agreement on the following scales.

A. For an eight candle power lamp, 12/ per year.
    ,,   ,, sixteen ,,   ,,   ,, £1 ,,   ,,

B. By demand indicator, at the rate of £1 per 16 candle power lamp per year, and charged on the greatest number of lamps alight at any one time, with 1/6 per quarter meter rent.

C. By ordinary meter at sixpence per unit, with a guaranteed minimum supply, and 2/6 per quarter meter rent.

J. E. RITTER.

Notice of prices to be charged in 1897

Street. The standard charges set by the Board of Trade at 13s 4d for any amount up to twenty units per quarter made electricity expensive, though Ritter offered it to his domestic users for 12s a year. This would have allowed an average use of two hours a day. Even this was beyond the reach of most, when an agricultural labourer in 1897 would only have earned from 3s 4d up to 5 shillings a week. Even a skilled tradesman on 12s 6d per week could not have afforded to burn two 24 watt lamps for a year.

In September 1897 the Gas Company reacted. They wrote to the Board of Trade in London drawing attention to J.E. Ritter's 'illegal' electrical works. Mr Cunningham, Secretary to the Gas Company, pointed out that Ritter had run the electricity across the street 'by unprotected overhead wires' and that he had 'put wires under the street.' He urged the Board to compel him either to obtain the necessary Order or to discontinue. A matter of nine days later Ritter sent his own letter of complaint to the Board. With some justification, he queried who had given the Gas Company authority to open the streets and lay pipes. He went on to point out that the Gas Company themselves 'pollute and poison the air' of the town 'with the 30% of their product which percolates through the leaks in their pipes.'

The letters of complaint flew back and forth to London and inspectors were sent out to visit Ritter's installation. Ritter persevered despite the opposition he faced and shortly before his death in May 1901, aged 48, he was providing electricity to seventy-five consumers in the town.

Ritter's wife, Mrs Elizabeth J.S. Ritter and her son, thirteen year-old Edward Stanton, then took over ownership and direction of the electricity supply undertaking. They set about continuing the developments John Edward had had in mind. Times were changing and gas was becoming more and more expensive to produce. In 1902 Mrs Ritter tendered for the lighting of the town streets at £1 a lamp. It seems the Gas Company must have lost their original contract to light the streets and when they put in a tender at £89, it was rejected. A Mr James McElwee offered to charge £66 75s per annum to light a total of forty-four lamps using oil. McElwee had previously held the contract and his tender was again found acceptable.

Mrs E. J. S. Ritter and
Edward Stanton Ritter

No doubt the Council took into account the fact that to have converted the lamps to gas would have cost an additional £50 and a very costly £350 to electrify them. Mrs Ritter was however asked to light the Town Hall clock with electric lamps which she did at a cost of £1 a year. She then extended the high voltage overhead line along the 'back walks' to the north end of Main Street and into Roeville, beside the railway station. This meant she was able to supply the eastern end of Main Street and Ballyclose Street.

In 1903 the Limavady Urban District Council purchased the Gas Company for £1,200. On becoming owner operators of the Gas Company they became no less unhappy with the electricity undertaking. The row continued through letters and legal consultations as the Council tried to obtain a monopoly for lighting the town.

While it was clear that according to the 1888 Act, the regulations were being 'flagrantly and continuously violated,' equally it seems the Council and their Gas Company had no right to a monopoly. More importantly, they had no power to stop the 'unauthorised and imperfect system' from operating.

New metal filament electric lamps were proving to be more efficient than the carbon filament type and in 1910 Mrs Ritter revised her prices to take account of this. Electric lighting still remained an expensive commodity at 12s a year for a 17 watt lamp and the price of the lamp at 2s 9d added further to the cost. The more powerful 35 watt lamp was even more expensive at £2 a year. A line on the revised prices notice mentioned that lamps could be obtained from Jacob Stevenson who had originally been employed as a carpenter on the Ritter estate. Jacob had proved invaluable to Ritter when he was setting up his electricity undertaking and his practical know-how would have become even more crucial after Ritter's death in 1901. In later years his son Jack would also work for the family in the Limavady Electric Supply Company. Jack would, indeed, go on to produce the draft 'history' of the undertaking which was eventually to be published by the Northern Ireland Electricity Board.

After the outbreak of The First World War in 1914 the electricity distribution system in the town had to be extended and upgraded because of an increase in the number of consumers. The gas undertaking was having serious problems obtaining coal. At the end of 1917 the company had one month's stock and had to close down for periods in 1918, operating only when coal merchants loaned small amounts of coal to the Urban District Council. Meetings between the Council and Mrs Ritter's two sons, Stanton and Alfred, were held in June 1918 and a detailed scheme agreed to extend and improve the electricity system in order to replace the gas supply. In September 1918 work was going well on 'new overhead lines on the streets' and by October most streets were being 'lit nightly with 100 power electric lamps.' These were times that John Edward Ritter would no doubt have enjoyed, had he lived.

He had offered to install electricity in Christ Church as far back as 1898 but it was his wife who was written to in 1917 to thank her for her generosity 'in supplying the electric light in the choir and chancel of the church without charge, since its installation in 1913.' Low voltage overhead lines had now to be erected in the town's main streets and two new substations built, one in Irish Green Street and the other in Lower Main Street.

Main Street at the turn of the 20th century. (An electricity pole can been seen on the left, at the bottom of the street)

The poles used for the new lines were made from red larch trees taken out of Ballycarton forest, Bellarena. A young Jack Stevenson saw them arrive in the cattle market by horse drawn timber cart. There, they were stripped of their bark, dried and treated with wood preservative. The cross-arms for the poles were made of oak from the Roe Park estate. With the bonus of Council approval for the system, demand rose steadily, requiring the need for an additional generating set to be installed near The Lodge substation. A weir near the Carrick Rocks was repaired and an old waterway restored to the Largy Green power station.

In 1923 Mrs Ritter decided to leave Roe Park with her daughter to live in Stroud, Gloucestershire, in the home of her late parents. Her son Alfred became land steward in charge of the estate and farm and his twin brother James Leslie, returned from the Army to take charge of collecting the electricity accounts. This was done once a week from an office set up in Main Street. Stanton Ritter managed the electricity undertaking by commuting from England on his Douglas motorcycle at weekends.

On the death of Mrs Elizabeth J.S. Ritter in 1926, the Roe Park estate, including the electricity undertaking, passed to her second son John Alexander, a major in the Royal Artillery. She had hoped Stanton would take over the electrical concern, but he preferred to continue his career in the Post Office Engineering Department in England. Major Ritter set about investing in the business. He recruited John T. Irwin, a qualified engineer to manage the electrical enterprise.

A former flour mill at the Roe Mill was purchased and overall generating capacity was improved. Five new substations were built, two in Catherine Street, one at ground level and one in an underground chamber beneath the footpath in front of what was then May's shop, on the junction of Catherine Street and Irish Green Street. Access was via a lockable iron grating and down a steel ladder.

Another substation was put in a brick building in the yard of

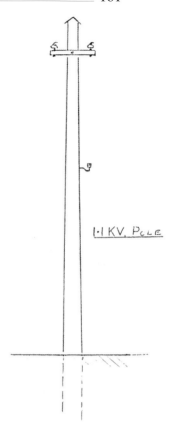

1.1 KV, POLE

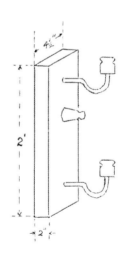

LOW TENSION

WALL BRACKET

Design for the poles

May's Corner

the solicitors' offices of Lane and Boyle in Main Street. Mrs Lane was Major Ritter's cousin, while another cousin, Dr Robertson, also of Main Street, allowed a substation to operate from his cellar. The fifth substation was situated at ground level in Ballyclose Street. Cabling now passed underground and, by 1927, electricity was available in Limavady twenty-four hours a day.

The possibility of using it for heating had been offered in 1920, at half the rates for lighting and in 1927 the company made it clear that 'ample power' was now available for heating, cooking, lighting and power. Three four-monthly billing periods were introduced per year, with special concessions attached to the 'summer period' which was counted as being from May to August. An attempt was made to attract those consumers wanting to use power by introducing three different rates for different types of usage. The enterprise continued to expand and evolve. Another substation built in Irish Green Street, known as Doherty's, was connected by underground cable to the Catherine Street substation. A 'Hire Purchase Wiring Scheme' for 'new consumers in cottage property' allowed houses to be wired and the cost paid off over two years. Typically, a 40 watt lamp, fully wired with a limiter, would have cost £3 at this time and the hire purchase initiative was obviously an inducement to widen the company's customer base.

When J.T. Irwin submitted an application for a Special Order in 1930, the general state of the whole undertaking was reviewed by a consultant engineer working for the 'new' Northern Ireland government. The granting of this Order would regularise the undertaking's status under the new Electricity Acts and give it authority to break open streets and so on, in order to lay cables. The consultant engineer concluded that the company had made a slight loss in the year ending March 1929, but that this had to take account of 'high capital charges and unduly large salaries.' On technical grounds however, there was no reason not to grant the Order and he saw good potential to expand the business. When Major Ritter died on 19th January 1931, aged just forty-two years, the Order had still not been processed and his widow was told to reapply in her own name, starting from scratch.

When Mrs Noel Pulleyne Ritter inherited the Limavady Electric Supply Company on Major Ritter's death, she retained J.T. Irwin as engineer and manager and her brother-in-law, James Leslie Ritter, in charge of accounts. Electric supply was now taken to White Hill and Gallows Hill and to Mr Lane's house in Ardgarvin. Drennan's pumping station in Myroe was supplied, with substations being erected at Myroe Road and Rush Hall and in 1935 Ballykelly was provided with electricity. Business continued to grow right up until the start of the Second World War. A showroom and offices with a workshop and stores were purchased in Linenhall Street. The premises included dwelling accommodation

J.T. Irwin

and this became Jacob Stevenson's new home. When James Leslie Ritter retired from overseeing the accounts of the business, Jacob's son Jack succeeded him.

The war meant that Northern Ireland became an important cog in the British war machine and the fight against Hitler's advance through Europe. A major part of the anti-submarine war in the North Atlantic was directed from Lough Foyle. Ballykelly became an important airfield in the defence of Britain and the growth of the base inevitably put demands on the local supply of electricity. The airfield was constructed in 1941 and where some two miles of overhead lines near the site presented a hazard to flying, they were put underground.

The necessity for this was highlighted when the step-up transformer at The Lodge burned out after a bomber crashed into equipment and overhead lines at Lisnakilly. Despite its important contribution locally, the Limavady Electric Supply Company was nearing the end of its life as an enterprise. On 1st May 1946 it was bought by the Electricity Board for Northern Ireland with all the Company's staff being retained by the Board.

John Irwin became the Board's consultant on water power and Jack Stevenson was appointed as the District Engineer for Limavady. J. T. Irwin's contribution is remembered in the Coolessan area near the former site of the Roe Mill, where a street bears the name Irwin Avenue. Ritter's Court on the Roemill Road honours the name of J.E. Ritter and his wife, as does a plaque on the power house building in the Country Park and the recently refurbished Ritter Tearooms immediately adjacent.

At the time of the take-over of the Company it had 1,095 consumers and thirty eight miles of circuits providing electricity to a population of around 3,000 persons. In 1897 it was one of the first places in the north of Ireland to have a public electricity supply and among the very first in Ireland to use alternating current. It was preceded by Larne, in 1892, Londonderry in 1894 and Belfast in 1895, although for some years Larne and Londonderry were only providing street lighting. The tiny Limavady Company had been to the fore in promoting the new technology for almost half a century. What is unusual too in the story of the enterprise was the close involvement of the females in the business. Unusual, because not only was it exceptional to see women involved in industry, but also because for most of this era women were still not even allowed to vote.

The Electricity Board continued to operate hydro-electric generation on the River Roe until 1965, but the scale of the business and the level of maintenance required to run it, were working against it. With the price of oil low, the Board began constructing a large oil-fired power station at Coolkeeragh, outside Londonderry and the arguments for using water power from the Roe seemed to weaken. In the present era, the search for alternative power sources and concerns over climate change, together with the rising cost of oil, seem to make the hydro-electric option available there, a fresh and innovative idea once again!

Limavady town centre in 1896

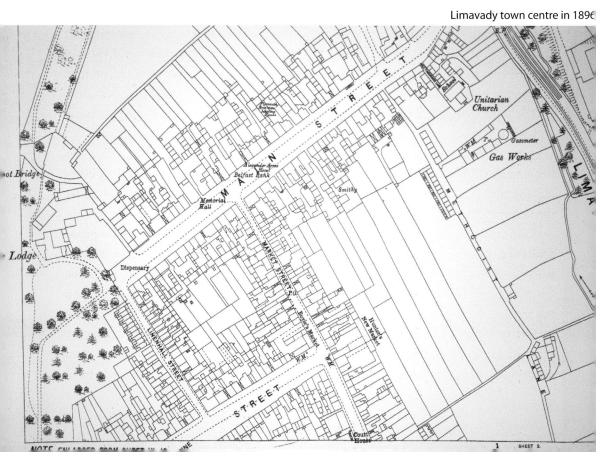

NOTE ENLARGED FROM SHEET IV 12   1   SHEET 2.

National Schools

As a result of the Reformation, the education system in England came to be linked to the Anglican Church. The Irish school system was remodelled along the same lines at this point, creating Church grammar schools for the sons of the rich, and 'petty' schools for the poor. In the petty schools the basics of reading and writing were taught, as this was considered sufficient for those who would only ever earn their living by manual labour. One of the intentions of the Plantation for our area had included the setting aside of 375 acres out of the monastery lands to erect a 'free school' at Limavady. This was never carried out, though if it had, it would have established a grammar school in the town then, with traditions similar to Dungannon or Portora Royal. As it was, Higher Education would not be provided for in the area for some time to come. In the following centuries many schools were set up by Charitable Trusts and Societies keen to spread their own ideas through education, but these catered for a very small section of the population. With the introduction of the Penal Laws in the 18th century, teachers had to be regular and practising members of the Church of Ireland. Subsequently, illegal 'hedge schools' were set up in out-of-the-way places to meet a growing demand for education. By 1824 there were 7,500 of these in the country with an estimated 400,000 children being provided a curriculum of basic reading, writing, arithmetic and sometimes Greek and Latin. With few books, a lot of this learning was oral. From 1786 the Sunday School movement started with the opening of a school at St Catherine's Parish in Dublin, which provided spelling, reading and a Church service. Other schools at the time, which made up this varied educational mix, were Royal schools, parish schools, diocesan schools and charter schools.

A bewildering choice of instruction became available in Limavady. John Lilly was the officially recognised schoolmaster in Drumachose parish in 1686 with James Forbes and Hector Smith recorded as holding the dual offices of Parish Clerk and schoolmaster in 1718 and 1767. Soon though, there were many small schools both in Limavady and in the countryside around it, with teachers who came from a variety of denominations. At Mullan's school in Killybready, which had cost £10 to erect in 1775, the parents of children who attended paid the master there a salary of £8 per annum. In Rathbradymore Jane Given, a Presbyterian lady, ran a school in a kitchen where the pupils brought in 1½d per week and a turf a day for the heating. Twenty pupils attended the kitchen of James McGrotty, a Roman Catholic, teaching in Ballyclose Street. In Main Street, the eighty year old Unitarian James Stephenson, said to have been a teacher for fifty years, had eighteen pupils in a rented room and was earning the tidy sum of £12 per annum from this. The Methodist Society had set up a school for the poorest children, in a thatched cottage measuring sixteen feet by twelve feet. The Methodist teacher Matthew Pollock was paid £26 per annum to teach the one hundred and one children. The parents paid ½d per week and the school was attended by thirty-one Church of Ireland children, ten Roman Catholic children and fifty-seven Presbyterian children.

At the parish school in the Glebe on the road to Garvagh, twenty of the forty-eight pupils who attended had to be taught free of charge. Built in 1817 by a grant from the Erasmus Smith fund, the schoolmaster taught thirty boys and eighteen girls made up of forty-four Presbyterian children, three Church of Ireland and one Roman Catholic. His salary of £20 per annum was met by the Erasmus Smith fund. Select schools were also available in the area in the 1830's. James Wilson, a Presbyterian, had a select day school in Main Street with twenty-one pupils and an income of £45 per year. Mrs Armstrong, the wife of the Methodist minister, ran a select school in the parlour of a private house specifically for the daughters of shopkeepers, charging half a guinea per quarter. In an upper room of a private house in Main Street, Covenanters Jane and Mary Dick ran a preparatory school for 'respectable children of both sexes.' The English and Classical Seminary established in 1830 by the Roman Catholic Patrick O'Hagan, was well attended. His sixty-nine pupils brought him an income of £80 a year.

Of the many Societies throughout Ireland which had grown up and which were receiving grants from the government, the most important and famous was 'The Society for Promoting the Education of the Poor.' Set up in 1811 by a number of Dublin philanthropists, with the help of Joseph Lancaster an educationalist, the Society became known as the Kildare Place Society. By 1831 it was educating 140,000 children, assisted by a government grant of £30,000. Around this time questions began to be asked as to whether it was still promoting truly non-denominational instruction. When it became clear that it was allowing controversial books to be used and that it was 'preaching' in its schools, the Society began to lose the support of the Catholic population. A new Board of Education had come into being in Ireland in 1831. The Board had seven Commissioners, one from each denomination, and had been given the task of setting up a national system of primary education and administering government grants. The new Board wasted no time and quickly withdrew the grants from the Kildare Place Society.

The Board's intention was that the new system would provide national secular education for all children between the ages of six and twelve years. Religious instruction was to be left separate from this, for the clergy to provide outside normal school hours. The Board offered a grant of up to two thirds of the cost of building a schoolhouse, with the local parish being expected to provide the other third. It was stated that it was preferable that this building would not be on ground connected to a church or a meeting house. In Limavady's case, neither the Ogilby Trust National School at the bottom of Main Street, nor the Termoncanice Schools on Irish Green Street, seem to have followed this request however. The nearest neighbour of the Termoncanice Schools is St Mary's Church, while the Ogilby Trust sits in the shadow of Christ Church.

Ballyveridagh National School near Ballycastle, Co. Antrim, serves as a good example of the new system in operation. It cost the Commission £92 13s 4d with local contributions providing £62 18s 5d. In 1850 a further £55 8s 5d was needed to build a wall for the schoolyard and for some repairs. This particular school was moved, stone by stone, to the Ulster Folk and Transport Museum, where it forms part of a reconstructed Ulster village. It was originally intended that a great deal of the cost of operating the schools would be raised locally, but the main source of funding was central government. The Board would make grants towards the furniture of school houses and to the payment of teachers' salaries and would provide books and other requirements, at half price, in addition to an issue of 'free stock.' While it was of crucial importance that the system bring together children of all faiths, between 1831 and 1870 the three main denominations struggled to make the non-denominational aspects of instruction acceptable to their own particular viewpoints.

Ogilby Trust National School

TIME		JUNIOR DIVISION	SENIOR DIVISION
From	To	First and Second Class	Third, Fourth, Fifth and Sixth Classes
10.00	10.30	Arithmetic	Home Lessons
10.30	11.00	Home Lessons (First Class Read)	Arithmetic
11.00	11.30	Arith, Tables, on Mon, Tues & Wed, Spelling, Thurs, Fri.	Reading
11.30	12.00	Reading	Writing
12.00	12.30	PLAY	
12.30	1.00	Copying from Books	Arithmetic
1.00	1.30	Arithmetic	Dictation
1.30	2.00	Writing	Reading Grammar,Wed
2.00	2.30	Reading	Geography, Mon, Tues, & Wed, Grammar, Thurs, Fri.
2.30	3.00	RELIGIOUS INSTRUCTION	
3.00	4.00		Extra Instruction For Senior Class Only

A typical National School timetable

The Church of Ireland founded many Church Education Society schools outside the national system and in 1859 the Catholic Hierarchy tried unsuccessfully to get grants to set up a separate Catholic system. Although The Powis Report of 1870 accepted that there were many schools in certain areas that did educate children of different faiths together, it also acknowledged that the system was, by then, largely a denominational one.

With the new national system in its infancy inevitably there were many shortcomings. One of the biggest problems was that there was a shortage of trained teachers. The profession was very poorly paid in comparison with other occupations and teachers often moved to other jobs when they had the opportunity. Hugh Downey, the first teacher in Ballyveridagh, was paid £5 per half year until September 1840 when this was raised to £7 and 10 pence. This was well short of the £25 a year given to Mrs Murphy, the Limavady Workhouse Matron, and well adrift of the wages of the Workhouse Master or Workhouse Medical Officer, who were each paid £40 a year. Indeed the wage is more in line with the average 10d a day earned by a labourer at the time. The collection of school fees could supplement this wage, but in 1855 in Ballyveridagh's case, this amounted to £1 in 1855 and £10 in 1861.

Entry into teaching was quite long and drawn out. It usually involved spending a number of years as a monitor or pupil-teacher in an ordinary national school, then six months as a student teacher in a model school. After this, two years were spent as a paid teacher in an ordinary national school. More training then had to be undertaken at Marlborough Street Training College in Dublin. As teachers, they were expected to lead exemplary lives, to keep accurate registers and accounts, and they were often required to keep their schools in good repair and provide the cost of the teaching aids from their own pockets. When Thomas Henry replaced Hugh Downey in Ballyveridagh in 1848, he was destined never to please the Inspectors. He was fined £1 10s because of the state of the school in 1856 and in 1875 he was fined £2 for erasing absence marks and warned that any future similar behaviour would mean he would be sacked.

Between 1872 and 1899 a proportion of a teacher's salary was subject to payment-by-results. This may have contributed to an increase in basic literacy and numeracy and in increased attendance, but it restricted the curriculum to that which could be easily examined. It probably also increased rote-learning and the tendency to concentrate on a 'bookish' learning style. It would be 1900 before a more child-centred approach and a wider curriculum would be introduced. The success of these changes, known at the time as the Revised Programme, was limited by a lack of funding. A great achievement of the national system however was the increase in the literacy of children over five years of age. This went from 47% in 1841 to 86% in 1901. While it is wrong to make comparisons across two very different eras, it is interesting to know that in Britain in 2004 only 78% of eleven year olds reached the standard expected for their age in English tests, 84% in Reading and a mere 63% in Writing.

The inside of a National school generally consisted of one large room where all the children were taught, despite the fact that their ages ranged from six to twelve years of age, or sometimes even older. Each age group was divided into sub-groups which would have spent half their time doing written work at their desks with the other half doing oral work at a 'draft' space at the front or side of the room, possibly under the supervision of a pupil-teacher or monitress. Each of these sub-groups moved from one activity to the other every half hour when a handbell was rung by the teacher. Since about half of the children would have been at 'draft' spaces at any one time, there was no need to have a place at a desk for every child on the roll. Added to that was the fact that attendance was very poor anyway.

Discipline was strict in National Schools partly because of the attitudes of the time, and to some degree also, because it would have been chaotic otherwise, given the different age groups and levels of ability. Corporal punishment was frequently used, both for correcting misbehaviour and for discouraging mistakes in schoolwork. The experiences of pupils seem to have been remarkably similar across the whole of Ireland, prior to Partition at least.

Page from Copy Book used in a National School

Furniture in the schools varied little, although schools in very poor areas would have been less adequately equipped. They would have had earthen floors and would have had fewer windows than schools in richer areas. It seems from the Ordnance Survey Memoirs that the National Board schools were highly unpopular in the Limavady area with the preference here being to maintain schooling by private subscription and to avoid any necessity for connection with the Board.

The Ogilby Trust National School in town was constructed in 1897 by the builder James Wray on a site donated by a wealthy landowner, Captain Ogilby of Pellipar, Dungiven. In an unpublished essay on the Ogilby School, Moya Richards writes how it is recorded in the Christ Church Minute Book that a few brick courses of the building had to be pulled down during the construction. The reason was that they had been built of local Limavady brick instead of 'best Belfast brick' as stipulated in the plans. In 1910 there were eighty-six pupils on the Roll with the average attendance being seventy-four pupils. In 1914 the teachers were Mr and Mrs H.J. Phillips. Moya Richards refers to Mr Phillips being the recipient in 1922, for the third time, of the Carlisle and Blake Premium. The much coveted county wide prize, awarded for efficiency, was worth £5, but it did not prevent Mr Beamish, the inspector, from conducting his regular visits. In an annual inspection in February 1923, Mr Beamish rated both Henry and his wife Agnes as 'highly efficient' and considered the Junior Assistant Mistress, Miss Susan Richardson, as 'efficient.' His general report stated that the 'substantial increase in attendance has justified the appointment of an extra assistant as from January last.' While he felt she was not 'robust in her methods' with her Infant groups, he did accept that she was 'earnest and works hard.' He also referred to the fact that the outside paintwork needed freshening up! In November 1923, he returned again. While again rating the teachers as 'highly efficient' he added that the work of the Principal and his wife was 'deserving of high commendation for skill and thoroughness.' The teaching of the Infants was considered to be 'generally good,' though 'spelling was weak and their reading should be better. Order was well maintained.' The Ogilby had one hundred and two pupils on the Roll in 1962 when it was eventually classified as not economically viable to bring up to standard. It was later replaced by Drumachose Primary School, but the building continues to be used to the present day for various groups such as Guides and Scouts. Even in a slightly tarnished state, the school is an imposing and attractive addition to the character of the town. Mr William Cook, who became Headmaster of the Ogilby in 1958, was to be its last Headmaster and then the first Head of the new Drumachose Primary School when it was opened on the 10th May 1971 by Sir Dennis Blundell, High Commissioner for New Zealand. The school's five teachers also transferred with Mr

Cook to the new school.

At the other end of the town, built on Irish Green Street and named after St Canice, the Termon-Canice Schools opened in 1886. The parish raised money for this in many different ways. A subscription dinner for example, was held on the 25th January 1887, which contributed eighty guineas. The Isle of Man schools that had served the community up until this, were then sold for £50 and tenders sought by the parish priest, Father McKenna, for the construction of a teacher's residence. The first principal seems to have been Mr Hugh Graham with Mr John Rea recorded as the principal in 1909. When this building was replaced by a modern school, it was eventually renamed Bethany and was used until quite recently by community groups. Sadly it is now in need of some repair and is at risk of becoming another part of our built heritage that could be lost forever.

The present day Bellarena Primary School is a good example of a rural National School. It was built in 1861 by the local landlord, Sir Frederick Heygate, and is said to have cost £500. Constructed in basalt it was built by his workmen, under the guidance of Mr Stewart, his stonemason. Mr James Doherty was the school's first teacher assisted

Termon-Canice National Schools

Bellarena School

by his wife Catherine and William McDermott, aged nineteen and a half. The Dohertys were paid £52 a year and lived free of charge in the schoolhouse, while Mr McDermott got £15 a year. It seems Mr Doherty also did the job of Postmaster for the area at the same time. The school was furnished with fourteen desks, each nine feet long, and eleven bench seats, a teacher's desk and chair, a fireguard, blackboard and bookpress or cupboard. On opening, it held one hundred pupils of mixed religion, 10% Church of England, 10% Presbyterian and 80% Catholic. Although fees were set at 8 shillings per year, two thirds of the pupils attended free of charge. From Monday to Friday school began at 10 a.m. and ended at 2.45 p.m. for schoolwork and then continued until 3 p.m. when Religious Instruction was provided. On Saturdays it ran from 10 a.m. to 11.45 a.m. for schoolwork and continued until 12 noon, to give the pupils their Religious Instruction.

Built in 1859 by the local landlord Samuel Maxwell Alexander, the Largy Primary School is the oldest primary school in the Western Board area. The attractive and imaginative design of the building remains almost unchanged on the outside since its construction, although the inside was renovated in 1939. The single classroom, which was heated by an open fire at each end, was connected to an adjoining two-storey teacher's residence. The tale is told that Alexander selected the school's prominent site by riding through his estate planting flags on every hill top to find which one was the highest. The entrance pillars and gates to the school, along with the building itself, are of special historical interest. The Largy Pillars became the main meeting place for the community to catch up on the local news and gossip and is the location of one of the very few Victorian post boxes still in use in the country. Research carried out by the local historian Elizabeth Moore has found that, prior to the construction of the purpose built school in 1859, a school associated with the Kildare Place Society had existed in the Largy area. This school operated from a stone built, thatched cabin house, from 1825 onwards. Mr William Reed and then Mr Robert Lennox, taught in this cabin house school, but the first teacher employed in the 1859 building which we have today, was Mr Alexander Robinson. He was to be described as 'a very excellent' teacher in 1863 and was commended at the time for his order, neatness, cleanliness and general efficiency. In 1878 Mr Robinson was succeeded by a Mr Marshall, who was in turn replaced by a Mr Campbell in 1887. Mr Campbell would remain teaching in the school up until 1920.

As a result of the Government of Ireland Act in 1921 and Partition, the National School system came to an end. From about 1924 the National Schools in Northern Ireland were called Public Elementary Schools. They were run by local education authorities, or by church authorities, with some government aid. Public Elementary

Largy Primary

Schools provided compulsory free education for children from six to fourteen years of age. There were no free secondary schools and only a minority of children, those whose parents could afford the fees, or those who could get scholarships, went to grammar schools. This would change after the Second World War, in 1947, when a new Northern Ireland Act brought in secondary education, making it compulsory for a child to attend school from five to fifteen years of age. An 'Eleven Plus' examination at the end of a child's primary education decided whether a child went to a Grammar, an Intermediate or a Technical school and by the late 1950's all pupils up to the age of fifteen stayed on in school. Today, free education up to Secondary level is the norm and the town is well equipped with a wide selection of excellent schools at all levels and also boasts a renowned third level college.

Limavady's 19th Century Built Heritage

For the moment, many of the former school buildings in the area remain intact or, better still, have been renovated and have come alive again, often serving as stylish family homes. This is not always the case in the borough. Not very long ago the town centre of Limavady was notable for the exceptional unity of its Georgian buildings. Like

Albert Terrace in Linenhall Street

The Lodge

the surrounding towns and villages, it owed much of its appearance to building renewal during the 1800's. This exceptional appeal has been increasingly threatened however as gaps are punched in the street fronts and replacement buildings alter the roof line, the look, and the feel, of the town. Perhaps this is something unique being squandered, or perhaps this is nothing more than another phase in the renewal of the town. To the careful eye however, there is still much that can be seen that dates from this past era.

Although Linenhall Street has undergone renovation to its 18th and 19th century buildings, the narrow street still retains a great deal of its character. The late Victorian Albert Terrace, with its elaborate cast-iron railings and gates, and bay windows, continues to bring a very attractive focus to the street. The unique square arrangement of the four principal streets and the rows of fine Georgian houses in Catherine Street and Main Street, which include the former home of the famous Jane Ross, help distinguish Limavady's town centre from most other town centres in Ulster. Taking together The Lodge from 1782, The Hermitage built in 1835 and Springhill House dating from 1840, it is still possible to get a sense of the undeniable elegance and richness of our Georgian past. On the other hand, at the lower end of Main Street, the listed, high Victorian houses from 1887 designed by W.J. Given, which added to this architectural elegance, are now long gone. Sadly they have been replaced by a boringly plain and featureless building that currently houses the local Lidl Store. Pulled down, at the same time, was one of the oldest buildings on the Main Street, the early low-roofed dwelling house that sat at the junction of Main Street and Connell Street. Some of these losses did not go unnoticed and the vigorous campaign to save the Town Hall seemed to show that the destruction of this heritage can still sometimes touch a nerve. A few remnants from this era though, have survived well into the 21st century and are still fit for purpose. Hunter's 1822 Corn Mill that now houses both the Oven Door Bakery and Supervalu, is a remarkable survivor. Equally remarkable is the old Roe Bridge, built in 1700 and enlarged in 1821. While it has been appropriately reinforced since, the bridge is still fully operational and more than capable of taking 21st century traffic.

Almost hidden out of sight behind the Shenandoah Bar, the former Railway Hotel, now occupied by Roads Service, is another beautifully maintained two-storey brick house from the late Georgian period. The churches too, in and around Limavady, greatly enhance the town's architectural character. The recently refreshed St Mary's Roman Catholic Church, built in 1836 of 'a pleasant rosy rubble or coursed sandstone' and designed by George Given, of the Given family of architects, is a noteworthy and beautiful asset to the townscape. The black basalt, Methodist Church, built in 1877 on

The Roads Service Offices formerly the Railway Hotel.

the same street, is equally charming and offers a strong contrast in style. Further down Irish Green Street, Second Limavady Presbyterian Church, which was built in 1840, is a solidly attractive building. Drumachose Presbyterian Church situated on what is now Church Street, is unusual in that it is built in a cruciform shape which is something that is very rarely found in Presbyterian churches. Setting aside its connotations, the Workhouse building from 1841 is one of the town's finest assets. As a building it makes a strong statement and a guided visit around it creates a very moving and interesting step back in time, not least for the tales of the ghostly crying of babies, of men and women appearing mysteriously in uniform, the unexplained knock on a window and the authenticated photograph of a nurse with her strangled baby.

Until relatively recently, one of the oldest buildings in the town centre, the town's former Court House, occupied a site on Irish Green Street. Dating from 1830, the building became the local Gospel Hall and was pulled down to be replaced by a new red brick Gospel Church, Church Hall and carpark. Robert Given is credited with having designed the original, classically-styled building and a short time afterwards is known to have prepared plans for a temporary prison to be erected 'adjoining the Courthouse.'

On the same street, opposite Limavady High School, sits a set of 19th century workers' houses. While alterations and additions disguise some of their original character, the two which are presently lying derelict give a good idea of their original size and brickwork. It

Workers' cottages Irish Green Street

Above: Sampson's Tower

Below: Ballyquin Beresford's monument

is difficult now to imagine an average family of nine or ten people growing up in the small space they afford.

Even on the perimeter of the town, unusual and intriguing vestiges from the 19th century period are to be found. Despite the fact that landlords are not generally given a good press in this particular period, two local landlords had monuments raised in their honour and memory at this time. Interestingly too, both monuments were paid for by public subscription. The year after his death in January 1859, Sampson's Tower was built in memory of Arthur Sampson, who had been the Fishmongers' agent for nearly forty years. Roughly eighteen metres high, the rubble and sandstone square tower has a circular stairwell giving access to the roof. At one point the tower was looked after by a 'guardian' who lived in a nearby cottage. Located on private land not far from the Rough Fort, the tower is difficult to pick out through the surrounding trees. There are, nevertheless, spectacular views over the Lough and countryside from the top of it.

Similarly, at Ballyquin, an obelisk known as the Beresford Monument, was erected on the 28th June 1840 by tenants to honour the 'virtues' and 'talents' of their agent the Marquis of Waterford, Henry Barre Beresford. Plaques on the monument further record that he was born on 25th of September 1781 in Walworth House and died on the 15th December 1837 in London.

Several bridges in the locality were rebuilt during this period. The Largy or Dog Leap Bridge was rebuilt in 1828 at a cost of £4,000, while Drummond Bridge goes even further back, dating from 1821. Artikelly Bridge was reinforced prior to the construction of the by-pass, but retains much of its original form which goes back to 1831.

All of the town's valuable past is not just to be found on the surface. Older residents talk of a set of tunnels that ran from under the Roemill Road to The Lodge, and down Main Street to an entrance, or an exit, in the grounds of the

Ogilby School. Their original purpose is open to debate, but it is claimed the section under the Roemill Road was once used to store whiskey from the distillery, in cool conditions. It has also been claimed the tunnels were built in order to hide the whiskey from Customs men. Some have said the tunnels were built to provide a secret escape route for the inhabitants should the town ever come under attack. Perhaps they carried drinking water through the town, or perhaps they carried rain water, or even sewage, away from the town. Certainly most of the houses on Main Street had, and indeed some still have, expansive cellars which extended beyond the house itself and out under the footpaths. The cellar of a typical house in Lower Main Street had space for a kitchen under the house and two large storage rooms which could be accessed from the footpath by a manhole cover or a grill. Perhaps these were the tunnels. Few in Limavady have ever really seen them and for the moment we just do not know why they are there, or how far they extended. So it is that, the puzzling mystery of the Limavady tunnels still remains, unsolved.

In common with many places across the province, scant attention has been given to important aspects our local heritage, such as these. It is striking how many times across the centuries people passing through the Limavady area record the pleasure they have taken, not just from the town's natural setting, with its magnificent valley and the Foyle estuary, but also from the unique attraction the town itself presents through its unity of architectural style. These key aspects have always had an exceptional appeal to outsiders and have always left them with a very positive and enduring impression of our area.

William Ferguson Massey, Prime Minister of New Zealand

Of the many notable men and women associated with the borough, one of the most eminent is undoubtedly William Ferguson Massey, who was born in Limavady on 26th March 1856, the son of John and Marian Massey. When William was just six years old, in 1862, his parents emigrated to New Zealand and he was left in Limavady to be raised by his maternal grandparents, Mr and Mrs W. Ferguson. At the age of fourteen he set off to join his parents in New Zealand where he began working as a farm hand, initially on his father's farm. In time, he was able to afford to purchase a thresher and to lease one hundred acres in Mangere. In 1882, he married Christina Allen Paul, a neighbour's daughter and the couple went on to have seven children. Massey quickly came to prominence in his adopted home, becoming a member of the Mangere Road Board, Chairman of the School Committee and, in 1890, President of Mangere Farmers' Club. He also found the time to be an active member of the debating society and to join the Freemasons and the Orange Order. Massey's keen interest in rural and farming matters, along with his involvement in Farming Associations, began to edge him towards the political scene in New Zealand. Soon he was working against the Liberal Party government of Prime Minister John Ballance, who was in fact, a fellow Ulsterman.

In 1890, at his second attempt to enter politics, Bill Massey, or Farmer Bill, as he was often called, successfully contested a vacant seat at Waitemata. Six years later he went on to run for, and win, Franklin district. A formidable and skilled politician it was a seat he would retain without interruption for the next twenty-nine years. On entering Parliament, he took his place on the opposition benches with the independent Conservatives. Massey saw the need to revive the Party's fortunes. He created a new conservative grouping in 1909 called the Reform Party, which had its roots in the conservative Political Reform League he had led since 1903. This transformation proved to be a successful political move and one which brought the Reform Party close to power. In the 1911 elections it gained more seats than the Liberals, but remained in opposition, having fallen just short of an absolute majority. The Liberals struggled to continue on however and soon fell to a vote of 'no confidence.' They were then replaced by Massey's Reform Party after the 1912 elections. Limavady man, William Ferguson Massey, was sworn in as Prime Minister of New Zealand on the 10th of July 1912 and would remain Prime Minister for the next thirteen years.

Massey had hard decisions to make from the outset. Although his incoming administration brought to an end that of Sir Joseph Ward, he nevertheless chose to continue Ward's policy of increased spending on defence. As might have been expected though, amongst the first Acts Farmer Bill's government pushed through, was one which enabled around 1,300 tenant farmers to purchase their own farms. The first months of his Premiership saw him tackling bitter industrial disputes. This led to him bringing in tough anti-strike legislation. His use of force to deal with the miners' and waterfront strikes of 1912 and 1913 quickly made Massey a figure of hate for the emerging left wing in New Zealand. He could however count on the support of the conservative-minded in the country who tended to believe, and fear, that the unions of the day were controlled by socialists and communists. It was during these strikes that Massey deployed Special Constables in order to protect non-union labourers. Liked and disliked in equal measure, these Special Constables became known somewhat ironically as 'Massey's Cossacks.' The outbreak of the First World War however diverted attention away from domestic matters. When Britain went to war with Germany in August 1914, New Zealand was in a strong position to lend her assistance. A Defence Act of 1909 introducing compulsory military service had greatly bolstered New Zealand's military efficiency. Internally though, the 1914 elections had left the country with a political stalemate. Neither Massey nor his opponents had a clear enough majority to be able to govern effectively. As Prime Minister, Massey reluctantly opted to share the responsibility of government with a coalition grouping.

A new National Government was duly set up in 1915 in which Farmer Bill served as both Prime Minister and Minister responsible for Lands and Labour. The Leader of the Liberal Party, Sir John Ward, became his Deputy Prime Minister. With Ward less than inclined to accept a subordinate role in the Coalition, the two cooperated for the good of the country, but did not always work easily together. During the war period they travelled several times to the United Kingdom, at the invitation of the British Government, to discuss military cooperation as part of the Imperial War Cabinet. On the very first of these visits Massey was accused of undermining the military leadership's official line because he was listening to the complaints of the New Zealand troops he went to see. While Massey was determined that his country would provide full assistance to Britain, he nevertheless put forward a fully independent view from that of the British Government, throughout the war. Despite their political differences this was one issue where Massey knew he could count on the wholehearted support of Sir John Ward.

In a politically courageous decision for any Prime Minister, Massey introduced conscription to the country from August 1915, further boosting the resources of the already renowned New Zealand division. The country's soldiers were to see some of the hardest fighting of the war, in France and, most notably, in Gallipoli. When the war ended Massey represented New Zealand at the Versailles Peace Conference in 1919. Securing a suitably sacred Christian resting place for the Australian and New Zealand (ANZAC) soldiers who had fallen at Gallipoli was one of his first concerns at the Peace Conference. The events of Gallipoli had quickly taken on special significance in the history of both Australia and New Zealand. It was an issue though which would remain unresolved for many years to come.

The fact that Prime Minister Massey was one of the signatories of the Versailles Treaty was seen as being hugely important in New Zealand and was noted as a critical step towards the country's governmental independence. On the occasion of New Zealand subsequently being invited to join the League of Nations, Massey made the point that it joined as 'a self-governing nation within the empire.'

On the political front back home, Massey saw the need for change and dissolved the Coalition in 1919. He then fought the elections on a platform of support for farmers, stability and patriotism, all of which would be backed up by a programme of public works. It says much for his personal popularity that in the elections which followed the war Massey was given a working majority and was reinstated as Prime Minister of the country. During this period he was able to effect large reductions in income tax and a return to penny postage.

Massey had returned to his native Limavady in 1916 and was to return again in 1923. On his second visit to Ireland, he returned to a country which had been newly partitioned. This time he was welcomed at Stormont Castle by Sir James Craig, the Northern Ireland Prime Minister of the day. During his stay he was conferred with an Honorary Doctorate by Queen's University. As well as taking in a visit to Derry, Massey attended a Church service in 2nd Limavady Presbyterian Church on Irish Green Street, his family's traditional place of worship. This was marked by a parade in his honour, of the local B Specials, under Major R.M. Macrory and Lieut. Col. F.S.N. Macrory. It was to be his last visit. After ten difficult years as Prime Minister, Massey's health was deteriorating and in 1924 illness forced him to relinquish many of his official duties. He died in office the following year on the 10th of May 1925.

William Massey was the 19th Prime Minister of New Zealand and the second longest serving after Richard Seddon, who had served three months more as Prime Minister. In New Zealand he is remembered as a shrewd, highly skilled and tenacious politician.

Prime Minister Massey as Guest of Honour in the Alexander Memorial Hall on 25th November 1916.

Throughout his career he remained a strong supporter of conservative farming interests. Massey is also seen as a man whose talent as an administrator did much to bring New Zealand through the war and put it back on the road to economic recovery. Massey accepted appointment as a Grand Officer of the Order of the Belgium Crown from the King of Belgium in March 1921 and appointment as a Grand Officer of the French Legion of Honour by the President of France in October 1921, but otherwise he turned down offers made to him of knighthoods and a peerage.

Shortly after Massey's death, land was set aside as a burial ground for him and his widow at Halswell Point in Wellington. Public subscriptions raised £5,000 and the government contributed £10,000 to construct an impressive marble and granite tomb and memorial on the site. New Zealand's Massey University was named after him in a gesture which acknowledged the connection between the university's initial focus on agricultural science, and Massey's farming background and interests.

In Limavady, Massey Avenue, built in the 1940's, is named after him and denotes his connection with our town. A small memorial in Irish Green Street locates the general area, formerly known as Kennaught Terrace, where he was born. The town's most impressive tribute to Massey though is the two metre high bronze statue of him by the sculptor Phillip Flanagan which is situated in front of the Council Offices in Connell Street. At the unveiling in September 1995, carried out by the New Zealand High Commissioner and Mayor

Prime Minister William Ferguson Massey

Barry Doherty, Flanagan explained that he had "given Mr Massey an overcoat" in keeping with the age in which he lived and that Massey's raised right arm was intended to give the work "a little more meaning." A variety of plants of New Zealand origin have since been grown around the statue, further emphasizing the link between Limavady and New Zealand. The work is a fitting tribute, in his birthplace, to his considerable achievements. Erected almost exactly seventy years after his death the statue appropriately acknowledges the significance of this important Limavady man who rose from the humblest of beginnings, to the highest office in his adopted country.

Conclusion

THE COMING 20ᵀᴴ CENTURY would present the world with a new set of challenges. In the aftermath of the First World War, memorials would spring up in towns and villages across Europe to honour the millions who fought and died. The maps that were redrawn in the aftermath of this Great War would touch close to home. The new frontier that partitioned Ireland, would divide most of one shore of Lough Foyle, from its opposite shore.

With the coming of the Second World War, Limavady and the north-west was to become a key strategic base in the struggle to halt the advance of Hitler's German forces. Airfields would expand to cover an area from Aghanloo to Eglinton.

Less dramatically, other influences from the outside world would filter into the community. By the mid-point in the century, modernist architecture would slowly begin to impact on the town. In the 1940's the Roe Cinema would herald the arrival of a change that would later see both public and private buildings such as the Post Office, the Grammar School and the Cricket and Rugby Club, not just continue, but also develop, this trend.

The town's strong sporting tradition in everything from Gaelic to Cricket, from Soccer to Rugby and beyond, would often be highlighted as talented individuals in the area regularly pushed through onto the wider international stage.

In general, despite 'The Troubles' and the occasional 'sensationalist' headline, the town would remain a well integrated and close-knit community. This strong sense of community is something which emerges from the history of Limavady, from its beginnings, through to the start of the 20th century. It is a community which fought for its survival through tribal wars, religious wars and even wars between whole nations. The origins of the community itself have been moved and altered, burned and destroyed, built and rebuilt. From the earliest of times in the history of the island of Ireland, people have been drawn to the area in and around Limavady in order to live off the riches found here. The layers of habitation laid down by past generations have done relatively little to harm the valley and its hinterland. Some vestiges of their passing are still available for us to investigate, to study, to learn from, or just to admire.

The small but growing village that entered the 20th century would continue its path through history rarely noted upon by the outside world. Nevertheless it has a significant and remarkable past. It is a past which deserves much greater attention and scrutiny than it has had to date.

Our heritage in this corner of the north-west needs dusted off and polished up for a new generation to understand and appreciate, because it is unique in so many important ways. The proper scrutiny of such a proud and illustrious past can not only guide our current thinking, it can also inform us and shine a light on the road ahead. This past is not a foe to be feared, not a truth to avoid. This past is the lost history of an old friend, with whom, we all have shared memories.

Select Bibliography

Adams J.R.R. *The Printed Word and the Common Man, Popular Culture in Ulster 1700-1900,* The Institute of Irish Studies, The Queen's University of Belfast, 1987

Austin R. (ed.) *The First Settlers in Ireland, Evidence from Mountsandel,* University of Ulster, 1987

Banagher History Group *Historic Monuments and Sites of Banagher*

Bardon J. *A History of Ulster,* The Blackstaff Press, Belfast, 2001

Benbraddagh Magazine *(various issues)*

Boyle E.M. F-G. *Records of the Town of Limavady 1609 to 1808, (facsimile edition),* North-West Books, Limavady, 1989

Brannon N.F. and Hamlin A. *Dungiven Priory and Bawn Guide Card,* Historic Monuments and Buildings Branch, DoE, 1986

Buchanan G. *The Poor Shop and Printing in Limavady*

Bunn A.V. *Dungiven Days,* Dungiven, 1978

Camblin G. *The Town in Ulster,* Mullan, Belfast, 1961

Causeway Museum Service, *Limavady Heritage Trail*

Curl J. S. *The Londonderry Plantation 1609-1914,* Chichester, Phillimore and Co., 1986

Curl J. S. *The Honourable The Irish Society and The Plantation of Ulster 1608-2000,* Chichester, Phillimore and Co., 2000

Donnelly P. *The Great Church on the Roe,* Limavady Printing Press, Limavady, 1982

Donnelly P. *The Parish of Banagher,* 1996

Eager A. *Bibliographical Guide to Ireland*

Elder R.J. (ed.) *Electricity from the Red River,* Northern Ireland Electricity

Elliot M. *The Catholics of Ulster,* London, Pengiun Press, 2000

Evans D. *An Introduction to Modern Ulster Architecture,* Ulster Architectural Heritage Society, Belfast Litho Printers Ltd, 1977

Feeny Community Association Ltd., *North Sperrins Heritage Trail*

Feeney P. *The River Roe and Other Poems with notes. 1850*

Feeney S. *Mullan's Bar research* (unpublished)

Gill C. *The Rise of Irish Linen Industry,* Clarendon Press, 1964

Girvan W.D. *North Derry,* Ulster Architectural Heritage Society, 1975

Gould M.H. *The Workhouses of Ulster,* Ulster Architectural Heritage Society, 1983

Gribbon H.D. *The History of Water Power in Ulster,* David and Charles, 1969

Guthrie R. *Hilding Brig research* (unpublished)

Hamlin A. *Banagher and Bovevagh Churches Guide Cards,* Historic Monuments and Buildings Branch, DoE., 1983

Hegarty A. *John Mitchel – A Cause Too Many,* Camlane Press, 2005

Her Majesty's Stationery Office, Belfast, *Historic Monuments of Northern Ireland, An Introduction and Guide,* Belfast, 1983

Hill G. *An Historical Account of the Plantation in Ulster 1608-20,* Irish Universities Press 1970

Hunter James. *Landscape and Population Changes in the Roe Valley*, Northern Ireland P.R.O. in association with Limavady Local History Society, 1958

Hunter Jim. *O'Hampsey – The last of the Bards,* University of Ulster, 1998

Hunter Jim. *Ancient Road Through Magilligan,* Cranagh Press, 2001

Johnson J.H. *Population Movement in County Derry in a Pre-Famine Year.*

Johnson J.H. *Agriculture in County Derry at the Beginning of the Nineteenth Century,*

Lewis S. *Topographical Dictionary of Ireland,* Lewis, 1837

Limavady Methodist Church 1877-1977 *Centenary Booklet*

McCutcheon W.A. *The Canals of the North of Ireland,* David and Charles, 1965

McSparron A. *An Irish Legend of McDonnell and the Norman De Borgos,* North-West Books, Limavady, 1986

Martin S. *Historical Gleanings from County Derry*

Mitchell S. *The Land of the Roe,* Creative Press, 1993

Mitchell B. *Historic Eglinton: A Thriving Ornament,* Grocers' Hall Press 1994

Moore E. *Reflections of Life in Largy*

Moody T.W. *Irish Historical Studies 1938-39.The Londonderry Plantation 1609-41,* W.Mullan & Son, 1939

Moody T.W. and Martin F.X. *The Course of Irish History,* RTE. and Mercier Press, 2001

Mullin T.H. *Limavady and the Roe Valley,* Limavady District Council, 1983

Mullan C.P. *The Irish Poor Law at work in the Roe Valley 1839-1948,* L.C.D.I. Booklet, 1998

Ordnance Survey Memoirs, Parishes of County Londonderry, (ed. A. Day and P. McWilliams) Vol.9 *Drumachose,(1991);* Vol.11 *Magilligan,(1991);* Vol. 25 *Tamlaghtfinlagan,(1994)* Institute of Irish Studies

O'Brien G. (ed.) *Derry and Londonderry, History and Society,* Dublin, Geography Publications, 1999

Munn D. *Placenames of County Derry*

Phillips M.S.S. *Londonderry and the London Companies 1609-29,* H.M.S.O., 1928

Preedy T. *Parochial Accounts of the United Parishes of Drumachose and Aghanloo, 1880*

Public Record Office Northern Ireland *The Great Famine Education Facsimiles 1-20* 1969

Richards M. *Ogilby School research* (unpublished)

Sampson G.V. *Memoir Explanatory of the Chart and Survey of Londonderry*

Sampson G.V. *Statistical Survey of the County of Londonderry,* Dublin, Graisber and Campbell, 1802

Seymour and Knowles *Parish of Drumachose*

Smith F. *O'Cahan's Country, A Local Study in Depth,* Reprographics Dept. W.E.L.B.

St Canice Jubilee Committee *Canice Saint of the Roe Valley,* Limavady Printing Company, 2000

Thackeray W.M. *The Irish Sketch Book 1843,* Nonsuch Publishing Ltd. Dublin, 2005

Usitat L. *Linen: The Story of an Irish Industry,* Carter, 1957

Woodman P.C. *Settlement Patterns of the Irish Mesolithic Period,* H.M.S.O., 1985

Young A. *A Tour of Ireland 1776-1779,* (ed.) H.W. Hutton, Dublin, 1892